One Mom to Another

BE KIND TO YOURSELF, EMBRACE THE GOOD,
FIND JOY IN THE EVERYDAY

PCN: 2019900001
ISBN Print: 978-1-7329877-0-8
ISBN Electronic: 978-1-7329877-1-5

Cover photo by Malisa Twelves
Cover design by Looseleaf Editorial & Production, LLC
Interior design by Looseleaf Editorial & Production, LLC
Interior illustrations by Gianluca Martini
Elephant logo illustration by Eric Anderson

Too Dang Happy

SHARING GOOD WITH THE WORLD

One Mom to Another

BE KIND TO YOURSELF, EMBRACE THE GOOD, FIND JOY IN THE EVERYDAY

CYNTHIA ANDERSON

To Rich, Melanie, William, Stephanie, Eric, Daniel, Caroline, and Michael, without whom this book could never have been written.

Contents

Acknowledgments

There is a lot that goes into the writing and publishing of a book. There are skills and talents required that I do not have. It makes me doubly grateful for those that do have them and are so willing to share them with me.

Without editors, there would be no books. All authors need someone to tell them that the story is finished. No more last-minute changes or rewording any more sentences. A special thank you goes out to Leslie Horn with Keen Editing Service. Even though I suspect she has run out of red ink, her respect for words and the stories they tell has allowed my voice to be heard. At the same time, she helped me follow the grammar rules and clear away all the extra words that were drowning out my voice.

Thank you to Kristy G. Stewart with Looseleaf Editorial and Production, who took all of Leslie's hard work and made it look pretty on the page and on the cover. Her formatting of the illustrations and other artistic touches produced a beautiful package for my stories.

Thank you to Malisa Twelves, who took the cover photo for my book. She was willing to drop everything, take and edit the pictures on a tight deadline during the Christmas season. Extra points!!

Thank you to Natalie Anderson and her children, Finn, Betsy, Jed and Archie for giving up a day to have their picture taken. Over and over and over. Natalie is beautiful inside and out, and her children were helpful and happy as always!

Thank you to Gianluca Martini for drawing the illustrations. Her illustrations add visual clarity to the chapters they represent. Her willingness to be patient with me as she drew the pictures that could only be seen in my head (and the amazing result) was nothing short of miraculous.

The biggest thank you is for my family. My husband, Rich, has been telling me for twenty years I should write a book. I didn't take this suggestion too seriously until one day, when I knew that was exactly what I should do. Soon after that, I announced to the family my intentions. Daniel then called me up and said, "Mom, I want to help you write your book." We started meeting together once a week. This soon turned into twice a week as we would read aloud my latest chapter, make edits, and bounce ideas off one another. I treasure the time we had working together, and am so thankful to his wife, Natalie, and their four children for letting me borrow him all those evenings.

I want to thank all of my children, those I raised and those that came into our family through marriage. From the day I announced my project, all of them have been tremendously supportive: giving suggestions for stories, insightful life events and topics. I am grateful for Eric, Anna and Caroline, who proofed and edited my drafts. Through all of their red ink, they would leave comments that expressed their love and excitement for the book. My thanks go to William for the many hours he spent setting up my website, taking pictures, and patiently helping me with whatever I asked him to do.

I think the greatest act of love from them all was, without question or hesitation, giving me permission to use every story in my book that I tell about them. As I would call them up and ask them "do you mind if" and then begin to tell them what I wanted to say, our laughing and going down memory lane together always turned into a lovely conversation. Taking time to see the stories from their points of view helped me to better relate the events in my book.

Love goes out to Rich, the love of my life, who has ridden the crazy ride of parenthood with me for forty years. Life is better with him; he holds my heart and I have no intention of asking him for it back.

CHAPTER ONE

Words I Never Thought I Would Say

"Don't blink, you will miss them
when they are gone."

*B*orrowing one of my favorite lines from an "American Idol" contestant cut from the competition: "What just happened here?"

That is the question I have been asking myself. When did I become that woman in the store who hears a baby cry and makes a beeline to the young mom with an arsenal of "helpful" advice? I hear things come out of my mouth like, "Oh, does your baby need a bottle?" In addition, I look at stressed out mommies and I want to hug them and utter the deadly platitudes:

- "These are the best years of your life."
- "The time passes by so quickly."
- "Enjoy your children while they are young!"
- (And the worst one of all), "You will miss them when they are gone." Aa-a-a-r-gh! When I do this, memories flood my mind of well-meaning older women giving me this kind of "helpful" advice and my reaction to it.

Certainly not my first experience hearing helpful advice, but one that stands out in my memory, happened in 1990. I was eight months pregnant with my sixth child. My good friend, who was about twenty years older than me, had called me on the phone. This is when phones were attached to the walls and the handset was attached to the phone by what is called "a cord." I invested in long cords, which enabled me to walk into another room where I might talk on the phone in relative peace and privacy. (A girl can dream.)

I pulled the cord into the kitchen, opened the door to the basement, and sat on the landing with the door closed over the cord, talking to my friend. My son, Eric, had followed me and as I sat, he was laying on my back with his arms tightly around my neck. Did I mention I was pregnant? I could hear sounds of destruction going on all around the house as the children realized there wasn't any parental supervision going on. I ignored the banging and the clanging, screaming and squealing as long as I could. (If they are making noise, they are breathing, right?) When I couldn't take it anymore, I told my friend I needed to go and assess the damage. Her parting words to me were, "Cindy, you don't know how lucky you are. The time goes by quickly. Enjoy your children while they are young." (Sigh.) I put the phone down next to me, rubbed my face with my hands, took a deep breath, and dove back into the fray.

I love being a mom now, and I loved being a mom when my children were all little. I didn't wish the away the time (too often). So, what is it about those helpful pieces of advice and words of warning that sound like fingernails scratching a chalkboard? After every encounter, I would say to myself, "I will never utter those words to a mother of young children. Never!" Well, how did "never" become, "Did I just say that?"

How it began:

It was 2012, thirty years since I had my first child. I had put my youngest child on a plane so he could travel to the great state of Oregon and serve a mission for our church for two years. All of a sudden, the day I dreamed of had come: I was an empty nester. I could read books all day, go to the movies whenever I wanted, I could eat a meal by myself, I didn't have to hide the soda pop or af-ter-school treats, I could stay up late and sleep in. No more schedules full of kids' choir concerts and soccer games, no more chore charts, no more midnight madness when a child remembers a homework assignment given two weeks prior and due first period the next day.

What did I do? Did I jump up and down? No. I cried. I cried and thought, "Where did those days go and what am I going to do now?"

I decided a little shopping therapy would help and so I went to the local T.J. Maxx store to buy a new purse. When I got to the purse department, I saw a mom with her two little boys. These cute little guys were trying to help her shop. It was important to them that she bought just the right purse so they kept bringing her different options and styles she might like. Each time they picked one up, three would fall to the floor. I just stood and watched. I felt the tears well up. This sweet woman looked at me and said, "Oh, no. You are going to tell me this is the best time of my life and I will miss this when they are gone." With tears coming down my cheeks, I said, "Yes! It's true and I am sorry but that is exactly what I am going to say!" I told her my story: seven kids; I sent the last one off today; now I am an empty nester, etc., etc., etc. I could hear words coming out of my mouth, while the voice in my brain was yelling, "stop talking!" But, my mouth kept making sounds. She was trying to pretend to be interested and polite. During this time, her two boys were running buckshot over the purse department and had started reorganizing the wallet section. She pointed to their handiwork and said, "And I suppose you think this is cute?" "Yes," I confessed and apologized again. At this point, she called her boys to her and held their hands a little tighter as she backed away from "the crazy lady."

I related this story to my daughter, Stephanie, who is a mother of five children. She said, "You all say that you miss this time of small children profoundly and that WE are going to miss it, but none of you, if given the opportunity, would go back or take on more children now." Well . . . she had a point.

After pondering these episodes from both vantage points, I have a few ideas that may help build a bridge from one generation of moms to the next: the truth is, something does happen to us when it is over. It's like that feeling you get when you have come through a challenge and, with great surprise, you realize all the things you learned on the journey. You see all of those tender mercies you might not have noticed before and realize that the hardships and hard days you survived did, as the saying goes, "make you stronger." Those days that seemed so long and difficult start to melt away in these realizations. You look at your adult children and realize your efforts counted for something. They move on and marry, they take care of and nurture their spouses and children, and although that is what you want, the days you spent wrestling on the floor, playing in the backyard, or tricking them into giving you sloppy kisses are missed profoundly. Somehow, in all those long years, the memories or treasures stored in your heart aren't quite as plentiful as you thought they would be. The tactile memory of arms around your neck and a child hanging off your back doesn't just warm your heart; it spawns a longing to feel it all over again.

When it's over and you realize the magnitude of the work you did with your children, you are left to wonder what could ever be that important again. What could you fill your life up with now that would have the same kind of meaning?

Then, we see played out for us, in living color, young mothers in the midst of the struggle, and we feel all of those feelings and we want to say to them, to you, "Hang in there. What you are doing is important and worth it." We want to hug you and tell you that everything will be fine. We want to help you see things from our point of view. There are so many feelings and emotions all jumbled up that it comes out in the awkward sentence, "Maybe they need a bottle." I don't know how else to describe it. We want to make sure you have enough memories in your heart and know that the day will come when you would give all you had to feel tight arms around your neck and wipe off a sloppy kiss and the only thing we can think of to say is, "Don't blink! You will miss them when they are gone."

Do we want to go back? No. But we want to help. We want to spread the good news that all is well and right and that there is light at the end of the tunnel. We want you to enjoy it and make memories with your children. Play a little longer at the park, let the dishes go, read more books together. Take a day off and do nothing but build sheet and blanket forts in your house with your children, go for walks in the park, and just talk. Cancel all of the to-do tasks of the day and take your kids to the zoo. Knowing that you will never have enough memories, make as many as you can.

And please, the next time a woman (and it might be me) tries to give you unsolicited advice about your children or starts crying and babbling in the purse department of a store, take a moment to give her a hug. One day it will be you.

CHAPTER TWO

That Time I Shut the Day Down

"A worldly construct cannot measure the eternal nature of motherhood."

*I*t was a summer day. I had six children at home, ranging in age from six to seventeen. My husband, Rich, had been out of town for a few days and would be for a few more. On this particular day, we all got up on the wrong side of the bed. No one could say a nice word to anyone, including me. I was impatient with my children and they were impatient with me. No one liked breakfast, lunch, or dinner. They complained when they had to go out to play, they complained when they had to come in. I said things to my children that shouldn't have been said. Finally, around 5:00 p.m., we were finishing dinner when someone delivered the straw that broke the camel's back. I had *had* it.

I called the kids together in the kitchen and announced that the day was over.

"What?"

"The. Day. Is. Over."

I went on to explain that it was clear that no one was speaking a kind word, and there was no patience or love being shown by any of us. Everyone, including me, was going to bed.

"WHAT?"

"Bed."

I told them they didn't have to go to sleep, but they had to stay in their rooms with the door shut. We would try to do better tomorrow.

"Can we go into someone else's room?"

"No."

"Do we have to put on our pajamas?"

"Yes."

"Can we brush our teeth?"

"If you are quick."

And so, everyone got into their pajamas, some brushed their teeth (I didn't bother to check), and we all went to bed. I felt awful. What kind of mother shuts the day down? I just assumed that only a bad mom would—that's what kind of mom: a failure of a mom. It wasn't true of course, but that's how I felt.

As a society, we measure everything from natural phenomena to sports statistics. Once evaluated, we assign some kind of number or rating to help us understand the event's impact and/or significance. Given this propensity to measure or compare things and events by a defined standard, it is not a surprise that we do the same thing with mothering. However, just as a seismometer would not measure air pressure correctly, the instruments we use to measure and then judge our mothering are inadequate.

I am not saying that there aren't standards or measures that we should try to achieve as mothers; what I am saying is that no one is going to succeed when using methods that employ some sort of binary measure like success/fail. A worldly construct cannot measure the eternal nature of motherhood.

Mothers need a unique, one-of-a-kind device that reframes our understanding of success, one that encourages individuality and leaves room for growth, not comparison. This tool should remind us what is important and help us and our family to continually grow and improve.

Perhaps because I love to sew and the things I use to measure are measuring tapes and rulers, I visualize a yardstick as a way to measure our success as mothers. A yardstick can be made from a variety of materials and comes with predetermined measurements marked out. However, I propose that we consider the idea of a mothering yardstick, made from scratch into a unique and personal creation that reflects the individuality of each mother.

Eternal perspective is the heart of our yardstick.

As we begin creating our "mothering yardstick," we give it a heart that reflects an eternal perspective. With the bigger picture in our hearts, the urgency of the world is dimmed, and we see our lives set into the context of eternity.

There is a story about three blind men. They were asked to describe an elephant. The first one touched his trunk and said the elephant was like a snake. The second touched his leg and said the elephant was like a tree. The third touched his tusk and said the elephant was like a spear.

I love elephants. I go and visit them at our local zoo and sometimes watch them on webcams in other zoos and sanctuaries. I have watched documentaries about this majestic mammal. I love watching them play and interact with each other in families. The children play and fight. The mothers in the group correct their behavior, feed them, and protect them. All over the world, elephants are revered for their strength, wisdom and loyalty.

None of these impressions or understanding about who or what an elephant is can be made by seeing a view limited to their trunks, legs or tusks. Seeing the whole picture in any given situation gives us creative insight and the ability to turn our attention from one angle of a problem to another. If I had had a mothering yardstick with the heart of eternal perspective on the day I shut down, I would have seen that my mothering was not defined by that event. Looking at the bigger picture would have helped me measure the day against an eternal plan and who I am in that plan. I would have been better able to move away from feelings of failure, trust in a good night's sleep, and be ready to try again.

Keeping an eternal perspective helps us get through the challenges of life. When "real life" events hit, our view may become limited to what is going on and we allow the big picture to slip as we are again constricted by a narrow view.

When my oldest son, William, was serving his two-year mission for our church in the Pacific islands of Micronesia, on occasion, when he was missing home, he would stand on the edge of the island towards the direction of home. His eyes would stretch to the end of the horizon, as far as he could see, and then in his mind's eye, they would stretch farther until he could see Hawaii. Stretching his eyesight further allowed him to visualize his family in Texas. There was comfort and peace in his soul when he was able to stretch his eyes into the unseen and "see" his home.

An eternal perspective, visible only through spiritual eyes, is often obscured by difficult circumstances. But if we stand still and stretch our eyes past our circumstances and then stretch them a little bit more until, with our spiritual eyes, we can imagine an eternal view, we can feel the peace that comes when we remember where "home" really is and that "God's plans for your life far exceed the circumstances of your day."[1]

It is easy for me to look back and see those years with my children living in my home with an eternal perspective. I better understand that some things I saw back then as important really didn't matter, and I treasure those moments with my children that did. But while eternal perspective gives us wisdom in hindsight, more importantly it can give us wisdom in the moment. We can better act according to our faith and belief in something eternal. We are reminded of who we are and our place in God's plan. An eternal perspective reminds us what we are fighting for. It helps us remember that "the things that swirl around us are not us and the demands on our life are not life itself."[2]

Eternal perspective corrects the notion that mothering is judged by some sort of timeline in which we will have a finite time to

---

1 Lou Giglio, *Passion, The Bright Light of Glory* (Nashville: Thomas Nelson Publishers). Used with permission.

2 Patricia T. Holland, "Filled with All the Fullness of God," *BYU Magazine*, Fall 1996.

mother and that at the end, there is some sort of judgment determining our success. Why do we think we have to have our children "done" by the time they leave home? Trust me: children will always need their mother. There will be opportunities for you to help, teach, and inspire no matter their age. "Yes, there will be moments of beginnings and moments of endings throughout our lives, but these are only markers along the way of the great middle of our eternal lives."[3] An eternal perspective reminds us every day that mothering does not have a finish line; no conclusions of success or failure can be drawn. Eternity does away with endings and tells us that we all have time.

Reframe our measure of success.

Our yardsticks now have hearts; they have been calibrated with eternal perspective. We are ready to add the units of measurement. When we reframe our measure of success to include the whole elephant, we can no longer make a judgement based on one day. No, the only real, trackable unit of measure is "movement." Instead of inches being stamped onto a yardstick, imagine all of the units are arrows moving forward.

Most years, Rich takes our children, William, Eric, Daniel, Caroline and Michael, some grandchildren, and sometimes their friends up to the Uinta Mountains in Utah. They put up camp along one of Rich's favorite fishing lakes: Wigwam Lake. Rich gets up early to fish and the kids go climb up the mountains. A favorite mountain of theirs is called Eccentric Peak. This mountain and others in the area don't have defined trails and are covered with large rocks. In order to climb, they have to find foot and handholds to help them balance and work their way to the top. After a day of climbing, everyone would come back to camp showing off his or

---

3   Dieter F. Uchtdorf, "Always in the Middle," *Ensign*, July 2012. © By Intellectual Reserve, Inc.

her cuts and bruises. They recounted the climb by talking about the times they "held on for dear life" or banged their knees or caught a foot in a rock. They talked about finding "just the right" rock to use to pull themselves up out of a hard place. The slips and falls are not proof of any kind of failure, but are part of the adventure, leaving marks they consider badges of honor. Placed in the context of moving upward, the challenges of the climb contributed to their success.

Everyone works as a team to get to the top. William, also known as "Mountain Goat," would lead the expedition. As the leader, he constantly helped the others manage the rocky surface and usually was the first to reach the top of the mountain. With his perspective at the top, William could see easier paths for those who were behind. Rather than sitting at the top watching them struggle, he would work his way back down, show them the easier paths, and help them find the best foot and handholds. William's success and skill did not cause the other climbers to be discouraged. They didn't sit at the bottom of the mountain not wanting to try because they would never climb like him. They learned from him and relied on him. This tradition that my husband started continued as grandchildren started coming. Those with more experience helped those who were struggling.

After the arduous climb, they would all find themselves at the top. Regardless of the order in which they arrived, everyone enjoyed the breathtaking view. They would celebrate their accomplishment, look out over the beautiful scene, and then carefully work their way down. It is interesting that as wonderful as the vista was, when recounting the climb, their narrative was focused more on the steps they took to get there, especially times they slipped, fell, or had to sit a moment and catch their breath. The view was the outcome of their journey: what they worked for, sacrificed for. It was the reward for "upward movement." At the same time, the lessons learned on the way up were not looked at as failures, but as part of the upward climb.

Like the slips and falls up that rocky mountain, the difficulties of life become part of our success as we continue upward, leaving the worldly view behind for a measure of upward movement that reflects the eternal nature of motherhood and families.

What we measure: prayerful family focus

Our mothering yardstick is taking shape! We have a heart and we understand that we measure in units of upward movement. The question needs to be asked: What do we measure? Under the previous system of evaluating ourselves, everything we do and say gets measured and judged. A mothering yardstick measures what you're doing against what you want to accomplish.

Families have distinct personalities. They have their own languages. They each have their "thing." It could be sports, music, board games, reading, puzzles, etc. Every family I have known has inside jokes that no one outside of that family thinks are funny. They crack each other up and have common memories they like to remember together. Families have life and religious philosophies that define a moral code. So, we quickly realize that no two yardsticks can be alike. It is from each family's own perspective, needs, and beliefs that our goals are made and upward progress is charted.

Rich and I had the "what will our family be about?" discussion early on in our marriage. Many things were talked about and questions like the following were asked:

- What kind of adults do we want our children to be?
- What is important to us?
- What is important to our family?
- What will we let go and what will we fight for?
- What lessons do we want our children to learn?
- What and how will we teach our children?
- How will we discipline?
- What is our personality? Sports, music, art, reading, etc.?

Using your own set of questions, you and your spouse (if that is your situation) could have a family discussion and then prayerfully take your ideas to the Lord. With everyone on board, our mothering, and what gets measured on our yardstick, will build around, support, and defend our family plan and focus. Because our plan is personal to our family, the obvious futility of basing our own family goals and plans off of another family's talents and accomplishments highlights the necessity of each family plan demonstrating creative individuality and unique personality.

For example, it was important to Rich and me that everyone in our family felt loved. This goal featured prominently on our yardstick. We wanted our children to know we loved each other and we loved them unconditionally. One of the simple ways I accomplished this goal was to try to greet the kids every morning with a smile and a silly song (many times, they asked me not to sing the songs, but I knew they loved it), and send them to bed every night feeling loved and safe. I felt like if they knew I was happy to see them in the morning, and if they knew they were loved and felt safe at the end of each day, I was moving up the mountain.

Was I perfect in this? If you read the first paragraph of this chapter, you would know I was not. But I had a purpose that drove me to accomplish this goal more days than not. The days I did not do as well evaporated away with the consistency of trying and continually moving up.

When we have faith and believe in the goals we have prayerfully set, it is the accomplishment of the goal, not our family's reaction to the goal, that measures upward movement on our yardsticks. For example, one of our family's goals was to read scriptures with our children every day. This was easier to do when the kids were younger. When we started having teenagers and busier schedules, we had to get creative. After looking at everyone's schedules, we decided that 5:30 in the morning was the best and only time everyone would be at home. Every morning, we would get up. And every morning, seven tired children would make their way to the couch. The younger ones went with it and participated, but we had at least one, if not two, sullen teenagers who did not go with it. At those moments they "hated life, scriptures, and parents" (not necessarily in that order). If I had judged my mothering by their reaction, I would have failed every day. But, the goal was to read scriptures every day as a family. Although it would have made some days a lot more pleasant, the children's enjoyment of that activity was not part of our goal. So, every day that we read our scriptures, upward movement was accomplished and I marked it as a success.

Our yardstick is made of adaptable material.

We have a heart. We understand the unit of measure and what or how to define what we measure. Now, we need to discuss the material our mothering yardsticks will be made from. Unlike a standard wooden or steel yardstick, our mothering measuring tool must be made out of the most pliable material that can be found. It has to allow for the changing ages and changing personalities of your children. It must take into consideration circumstances or events that turn our lives upside down. It allows for moves, job changes, and evolving seasons of life. It allows for the learning part of the curve. And on and on it goes. Life is like a baby: just when you get their schedule fixed, they go through a growth spurt or start teething and the schedule needs to be thrown out and a new one put into its place. If our yardstick is fixed and cannot accommodate the pressures of life, life will cause it to break. The upward movement will be stalled as we find ourselves slipping backward on the rocky path.

When Stephanie, my third child, was born, I was thrown for a loop. She was darling and cute and wonderful. But after she was born, I had a hard time. When I look back on it, I realize I had postpartum depression, and the realization that I had more children than I had hands made me feel outnumbered and overwhelmed. I couldn't figure out why all my days seemed to fall apart and nothing was accomplished.

When trying to come up with a solution, I (someone who loves structure, to-do lists, and a clear plan) didn't see anything wrong with the structure I had in place. I thought I was the problem. I decided that I needed even more structure: a more defined outline of what the day should bring would help get me back on track. I was measuring a successful day against my ability to stick to and accomplish everything on my list. After a couple of days of my "solution," Rich came home and found me in tears. "What is wrong?" he asked. I showed him my schedule for the day. It was written on a piece of binder paper with the times of the day listed on the left-hand side in 15-minute increments. Each line indicated a task to be finished. I was discouraged because I couldn't stick with it. I said, "The kids just mess it up every day."

I had to learn: children don't know the plan. Although I tried to impose some structure on the day, I learned I could not and should not try to live my life in 15-minute increments. I needed a new measurement that reflected the time of life I was in. It had to accommodate fluctuating hormones and a new baby. It had to forgive a messier house than I was used to. I learned to let go of my preconceived notions of what I thought a successful mothering day would look like, relax the schedule, and look at the day's list of to-dos more like guidelines. As I allowed myself to move through this process, adapting my plan for change, I learned that my goals could be achieved if I left my comfort zone and acknowledged there might be another way. Although I still loved a good to-do list and a well-plotted spreadsheet, I was equipped to measure my success with more kindness. I was able to move through the depression and come out on the other side with a stronger feeling of purpose, focus, and accomplishment than any to-do list or schedule could provide.

Armed with a loving, one-of-a-kind, made-just-for-us mothering yardstick, phrases like "bad mom" or "mom fail" cease to be part of our vernacular. Confidence replaces fear as we climb our figurative rocky mountain every day. Regardless of the slips and falls or the unknown challenges, we continue moving up and trusting in our yardstick to put the day into perspective. Our yardstick helps encourage us to keep moving, ask for help when needed, help each other when we can, and focus on what we accomplish. And, when the time comes that we find ourselves standing on top of the mountain we climbed, the words ". . . in retrospect, the years of struggle will strike you as the most beautiful"[4] will be reflected in the view.

4 Sigmund Freud and Carl Jung, Letters, German Edition, September 19, 1907.

CHAPTER THREE

When Everything Seems to Matter, What Matters Most?

"The frantic rush of everyday life can make us believe that it all matters."

*W*hen all my kids lived at home, I spent so much time in my car picking children up, dropping them off, going to games, concerts, assemblies, errands, and stores that I would have to say that Michael, my youngest, was raised in a car seat. During this busy time, I pushed myself at a frantic pace, relying on my dream of future days, when the children were gone, when I would have nothing to do and could enjoy a carefree, responsibility-free life. I thought I would wear myself out now and rest later. Wrong. I have come to the conclusion that in all stages of life, we find ourselves so overwhelmed with tasks, to-do lists and the busyness of life, that we spin in circles accomplishing nothing more than exhaustion.

"We can all think of a list of tasks that will overwhelm our schedule. Some might even think that their self-worth depends on the length of their to-do list. They flood the open spaces in their time with lists of meetings and minutia—even during times of stress and fatigue. Because they unnecessarily complicate their lives, they often feel increased frustration, diminished joy and too little sense of meaning in their lives . . . any virtue, when taken to an extreme, can become a vice. The wise resist the temptation to get caught up in the frantic rush of everyday life. In short, they focus on things that matter most."[5]

If we follow that wonderful advice, we must first answer this question: when it all seems to matter, how do we know what matters most?

---

5   Dieter F. Uchtdorf, "Of Things That Matter Most," *Ensign*, November 2010. © By Intellectual Reserve, Inc.

What matters most to you?

The "frantic rush of everyday life" can make us believe that it all matters; we embrace the overwhelming-ness of life as normal. But, the truth is, it doesn't have to be. When our calendars are full of school, work, and extracurricular activities, all screaming for attention, we get caught up in the notion that everything is a have-to or a need-to. First and foremost: you are in charge.

Once, I was having a conversation with Stephanie, who was around 11 years old. She had asked me if she could go play at her friend's house when the parents were not home. I told her she could not go. She said, "Lucy's (not her real name) mom said it was ok." I said, "Lucy's mother is not the boss of me."

When we are the boss of ourselves, we can act instead of react to the events that push and pull us around in life. With this perspective, we realize that not everything carries the same weight or requirement of fuss. We can create a balanced schedule that reflects us and our own individuality, circumstances, and abilities. Previously perceived "have-tos" can be modified or dropped from the list when we are the boss of ourselves.

When I was about 25, I was critical of someone I thought could do more if she just tried. The spirit chastised me and said, "Not everyone walks at the same pace." As life and my health have slowed down my pace, I am grateful for the understanding that the Lord does not judge or compare us to others.

"We women have a lot to learn about simplifying our lives. We have to decide what is important and then move along at a pace that is comfortable for us. We have to develop the maturity to stop trying to prove something. We have to learn to be content with what we are."[6] The world and its opinions don't have a place as you

---

6   *Glimpses into the Life and Heart of Marjorie Pay Hinckley*, ed. Virginia H. Pearce (Salt Lake City: Deseret Book Company, 1999), 74-75. © By Deseret Book Company. Used with permission.

opt in or out of any of those calendar items that align your family's schedule and obligations with you, your situations, and your stride.

What matters most to the Lord?

We can better bring into focus what matters most for our family when we ask the Lord what matters most to Him. As we draw closer to the Savior, we walk further from the unrealistic expectations of the world. When we understand how the Lord wants us to spend our time, we can further bring our lives into balance and better answer the question I asked at the beginning of the chapter: How do you know what matters most?

"In a world that thrives on comparison and competition, our souls yearn for one needful thing to bring the weightier matters into focus and provide clear direction for our hectic schedules today and all our demanding tomorrows."[7] It is easy to lose track of the things that matter most when the world is screaming at us to get our attention; how quickly this changes our thinking and perception.

A few years ago, I went outside after an ice storm, slipped on the ice, and pulled a muscle in my leg. It was very painful, swollen, and had a wonderful collection of bruises. It was about three days before I could walk on it. Rich insisted that I spend those three days in our recliner. Every time he would hear the chair creak, he would call out, "What are you doing?" Needless to say, visions of to-do lists were dancing in my head as I became a little grumpy at my circumstances and upset with myself for not being able to manage the fall a little better.

At first, I decided that it would be a perfect time to write a talk for a conference I had coming up. A conversation began in my head, "I should use this time to study for my talk. That is a great idea, but

---

7 Camille Fronk Olson, *Mary, Martha and Me* (Salt Lake City: Deseret Book Company, 2006), 2. © By Deseret Book Company. Used with permission.

I am going to see if there is a good movie on TV that I can record." A prompting came to my mind: "If you turn on the TV, that is how you will spend the day." I picked up the conversation in my head, "I am not a daytime TV watcher. I will be quick and get right to work on my talk."

Show number one was a talk show: "The View." There were about five women talking at the same time and I found myself less interested in what they were saying than I was in their makeup. "Why doesn't my makeup look as good as theirs?" I looked at the configuration of color and design on their eyes and thought, "I have tried that look and ended up looking like I had raccoon eyes. Why does it work for them?" I realized their eyes were huge. "Have they attached a magnifying glass on the camera lens? Who has eyes that big? If I had bigger eyes, I could wear makeup like that and I would look glamorous and beautiful. My small eyes ruin everything. If I had eyes that were four inches across, I would be beautiful."

Show number two was another talk show. I did not know the host, but she had Alyssa Milano on her show. You may remember her as the actress who played Tony Danza's character's daughter in the 70s sitcom "Who's the Boss?" Alyssa told a cute story about her son who sits on her lap while her stylist does her hair and how cute it is that when she takes him to get his haircut, he asks if they are going to his stylist. "Well," I thought, "that's how to have good hair. If I had a stylist, my hair would look good. I can never reach around my head as well as a stylist could. I wonder how much it would be to hire a personal stylist?"

I fell asleep and woke up to show number three, "The Ellen DeGeneres Show." Evidently, for 12 days during the Christmas season, Ellen gives away free items to her studio audience. I sat in amazement as everyone in the audience received over a thousand dollars' worth of free stuff! "Well, now, this is great. What if I ordered tickets now for her Christmas shows next year? I could stay in L.A. for all 12 days and participate in her giveaways every day!"

My conclusions at the end of the day were:

1. My eyes are too small.
2. The way to achieve good hair is to hire a personal stylist.
3. I was going to stay in L.A. for 12 days over Christmas just to receive free stuff.

By ignoring the prompting to turn the TV off, nothing that "mattered most" had been done. I made a choice that didn't include the Lord in my day and I allowed my focus to move from the Lord to the world. I was grumpy and upset with life. To deal with it, I entered the world for solutions and what I ended up with were problems and low self-esteem.

The best laid-out plan can become unbalanced as the pushes and pulls of the world continue to invade our home. If we include the Lord in our plan, He can help us stay focused on what is important and the world will hold no sway.

What matters most when the contrary winds blow?

The story of Peter attempting to walk on the water to meet the Savior is one of my favorites. You'll recall that Jesus had asked His apostles to cross the Sea of Galilee in a small ship without Him. During the night, they found themselves "tossed with waves, for the wind was contrary."[8]

Trying to manage the schedule of a busy home is hard enough when the "sea is calm." Trying to manage it when the "winds are contrary," as the trials and tribulations of life distract us and take over is very hard.

Two thousand five was an eventful year in our home. I was asked to serve as the Relief Society president in our ward. The first year I served, I had my foot operated on and my gallbladder

---

8 *The Bible: Authorized King James Version.* Oxford University Press, 1998. Matthew 14:24.

removed, all while working full-time. A short time after the gall-bladder surgery, the water heater in the attic (a Texas thing) burst at a welded seam. Rich had taken the kids to the Uinta Mountains in Utah on a backpacking trip and I was at work all day, which allowed the hot water to flood our home for six hours. After the initial assessment, it was determined that we would need to live in a hotel for what they thought would be a few weeks, while the repairs were being done.

Rich and I, Caroline, Michael, Oakley and Daisy (our two dogs), and Penelope and Cruikshank (our two cats) all checked into a two-bedroom kitchenette mini-suite at the Residence Inn. Daniel, who was still living at home with us, went to stay at his sister, Melanie's home. What was supposed to be a few weeks' stay turned into four stressful months, after which we moved into our yet-to-be-completed home. It took another four months of workers in our house every day before we had our home to ourselves.

As a portend of things to come, the night we were supposed to "move to the hotel," we let our Collie out into our backyard for a while. We did not realize the gate was open. Daisy decided to do a bit of exploring and after an exhaustive search on our part, was nowhere to be found. She showed up the next morning quite pleased with herself and couldn't understand why the humans were making such a fuss. Over the course of those first four months (July to November), Oakley had to have two emergency surgeries (two months apart). On a regular basis, Daisy would run out of our hotel room, up to the front desk and "do her business" at the feet of the front desk personnel. awesome. That is not the good "Awesome" with a capital A, rather the all-lowercase, not good "awesome."

Daniel went to college and I had to do all of the necessary errands and shopping as well as send off money for room deposits and utilities to get him ready to leave home. On the heels of that, Eric left on his mission, coming home from school with all of his earthly possessions to be stored in the small "living area" of our suite in the hotel. Eric and I managed the required errands, shopping and the necessary doctor visits. Family came in from out of town to see him off, all needing a place to stay. Looming in the future was Christmas. We had made a plan the year prior that I would host my family for Christmas, which included my mom, stepfather, all of my brothers and their families, my children and my grandchildren. Rich had a job that required heavy travel. When Rich was out of town, my daily schedule consisted of:

> 5:30 am: Caroline, Michael, Oakley, Daisy and I would leave for the day. I dropped Michael off at football and Caroline at seminary. I took myself and the two dogs to work at the Animal Hospital.

> 2:30 pm: I went to pick up the children, bring them back to work, where they would do homework in the break room until I was ready to go home. Most days, dinner was at a restaurant or take out place, or if we got to the hotel early enough, the hotel "happy hour," also known as the hors d'oeuvres bar.

On the approach of the fourth month, thanks to the contractor, our home had additional damage. Things that had been "fixed" needed to be redone. In addition, Daniel was off to school and I was missing both him and Eric, who had left for his mission. Everyone was tired of the hotel and our schedule. I was tired of juggling the children, my job, and my calling. Now, with it being November, I didn't know how I could host Christmas in a house without walls and baseboards. All of our possessions were crammed into three rooms. I couldn't see an end or resolution to our situation. I felt crushed by the weight of it all.

One Sunday, during this stressful time, my friend, Terri, came up to me after church and expressed her concern for my family, our situation, and me. After thanking her for the kind words, she asked me, "What tender mercies have you noticed along the way?"

I just stared at her. I didn't have an answer. Finally, I started to cry and said, "None."

After my friend saw my face and heard my answer, she assured me that I was not alone, and that she was praying for my family and me. The next day, she brought a home-cooked meal to feed my family (the best we ever tasted). With her simple question, she reminded me what was important. She reminded me that in my trials and stress, I could only see what was wrong. The "contrary winds" had changed my focus and I allowed my faith to weaken. And, like Peter who set out onto the water with faith and became distracted by the boisterous winds, I, too, took my eyes off the Lord, and also like Peter, I began to sink in the stormy sea.

When Peter felt himself beginning to sink, he cried out to the Lord. Immediately, Jesus caught him, and said those familiar words, "O thou of little faith, wherefore didst thou doubt?"[9] I think that is the most beautiful part of the story. I don't see the Savior's words as a rebuke, but an assurance that the Lord will always help us when we ask.

I tested that assurance and asked the Lord for forgiveness and for help. With renewed faith and resolve to recognize and be grateful for blessings, all I could see were tender mercies. During the second four months (November-February), my schedule seemed to work out better. Even though the repairs to the home weren't done, the contractor that was making everything such a misery was fired and the insurance company gave me a wonderful new company to work with. We were able to move back into our home and even though we had to work around the workers, I was able to once again take care of my family and return to an almost normal schedule. We were able to clear the rooms and, that Christmas that I had looked

---

9   *The Bible: Authorized King James Version.* Oxford University Press, 1998. Matthew 14:30-31.

upon with such dread turned out great. When everyone arrived, no one noticed the unfinished baseboards, damaged walls, etc. It didn't matter.

Focusing on what matters most even when the wind howls, takes the faith of Peter and a desire for the Lord's help. The howling of the world holds no voice. The winds, the rain, and the storms have no effect on Him who commands them all.

What matters most to your children?

I don't think I did much by myself anymore after I had my oldest child. When I was in the kitchen, doing laundry, sewing, going to meetings, I always had some assortment of children by my feet. Most children just like to be near their mothers. They want us to spend our time with them. Knowing that the time will come when our children's interests and age will mean that we have less time with them, what matters most is what matters to them: you.

Once, when Eric was in half-day kindergarten, I picked him up from school and told him we were going to see the movie *The Land Before Time* at the theater.

"What? Just us?"

"Yes."

"Mom, is this a 'psych'? (A cool word of the time.) It wouldn't be fair if this was a psych."

I assured him it wasn't and off to the theater we went. Spoiler alert: I will admit to being a bit horrified that the mother dinosaur died a violent death in a children's movie (it all works out in the end). But, Eric and I had what would be defined by both of us as one of our favorite memories. We liked the movie, but the thread that holds that memory so dear, so clear even after all this time, is the surprise, the spontaneity of throwing the schedule away and doing something unexpected together.

What matters most when everything seems to matter? This is not a simple question and has an ever-changing answer as we transition through different periods and stages of life. If we focus on what matters most to us, the Lord and our children, keeping our faith when things turn upside down, we are better able to ignore the distractions and wisely resist the temptation to get caught up in the "frantic rush of everyday life." We must remember to never sacrifice the things that matter most for the things that matter the least.

CHAPTER FOUR

You Can't Choose Your Children's Memories

"It is in the everyday that memories are made."

A few years ago, my daughter Stephanie and her children came home for their annual summertime visit. Her daughter, Avery, was a toddler at the time and she was sitting on my lap while I was singing her some songs. My usual repertoire includes, but is not limited to: "Ahhh-Goonk Went the Little Green Frog" (complete with facial expressions); "Round About Goes the Mouse;" "There Was an Old Sow" (also with facial expressions and various noises); "Popcorn Popping;" "Horsey, Horsey;" and "Kookaburra Sits in the Old Gum Tree." You get the picture.

After I had sung a few songs, Avery climbed off my lap and went to play. I looked at Stephanie and asked her, "Do you remember me singing those songs to you?" She replied, "No, did you?" I think she must have noticed my chin dropping and my eyes filling up with tears because she quickly added, "I remember you singing them to the younger kids." That didn't help. She quickly followed with, "If you say you sang them to me, I will believe you." With panic-laced incredulity, I turned and said, "Stephanie. Before bed each night you all got to choose a book and a song! We would sing during the day. We had a 'Pick Up Your Toys' song and a 'Rules Are Good' song. I made up a song when you all were grouchy or sad." I had to sit down. "Don't you remember any of that?" "No," she said.

Where did I go wrong? I had carefully planned it all out. I knew in the depths of my soul that they would remember and tell others about their wonderful mom who sang songs to them throughout the day. I knew it would be their favorite childhood memory; it would be what they would talk about at my funeral. And I would not even have to tell them to! During the funeral, they would sing the songs their mother sang to them as a tribute to her life of selflessness and sacrifice. Any mistakes I had made along the way would be forgotten, burned away by the shining memory of a mother who sang to them. I explained all of this to Stephanie. She, being a sweet and kind person, looked at me and said, "Um, I would be happy to mention it at your funeral if you would like." This would not do. Curiosity got the better of me and I asked her, "What is your favorite childhood memory of me?" Her answer gave me my second shock of the day. She said it was the day we had a blizzard come through and it was really cold and snowy. It was on a Monday; it was supposed to be the first day back to school after Christmas break, but because of the weather, school had been cancelled. She remembered playing in the snow and sledding down our backyard hill with me and her brothers and sisters. Of all of her childhood memories with me, that was her favorite.

After the room quit spinning and I gained some composure, I explained the following: I did not like that day AT ALL. (Yes, "at all" needs to be in caps.) It wasn't the kids, it was me. We had just finished a two-week Christmas break, which included bad storms that kept the children in the house for the better part of the two weeks. The blizzard that hit the day the children were supposed to go back to school was worse. It dumped 12 inches of icy snow and "the people" who are in charge called a snow day! Which, in fact, turned into a snow week, giving the kids (lest you missed this), a three-week Christmas break.

All that morning, the kids fought with each other. When I told them to "go play," they would look at me and say those dreaded words, "I'm bored." My response was to send them outside. The grumbling and mumbling would begin as I helped the children on with their snowsuits, scarves, hats, gloves, and boots. "Have fun!" I called out as I closed the door to complaints. Literally. They were complaining and, mid-sentence, I closed the door. They yelled through the door, "No one else's mother is making her kids play outside!" "Well, no one else's mother is as nice as I am," I replied.

But since I was inside and not yelling, they didn't hear me. Probably for the best.

It wasn't like I was sending them out with nothing to do. We lived in the Midwest, where there are no fences between yards. Starting at the top of our neighbors' yard was a large hill that extended down to our back porch, making it a perfect sledding hill, creating hours of play. We had a large retaining pond across the street from our house that was frozen solid. They could play hockey, ice skate, and go sledding down the banks of the pond onto the ice. There were plenty of things for them to do. Each time they went out, they lasted about ten minutes and then the complaints increased in volume. "We are getting frostbite," "It's too cold," "No one else is outside," and "We want to come back into the house!" You get the picture. And, back in they came. All the snow gear: snowsuits, hats, gloves, mittens, scarves, and boots, were taken off and put into the dryer. I had peace for a few minutes until boredom set in and the fighting began again. "Go get your coats and things out of the dryer!" This cycle repeated itself for most of the morning.

After the last round of cabin fever, I couldn't take it anymore, I proclaimed, "Everyone go get your snow gear. We are all (including me) going out to play for a mandatory one hour." As Stephanie described, we played in the snow, took the sled out of the garage, and took turns riding down the hill in our backyard. And when the hour was up, we all went inside. After that, I let the kids put in a movie as I made dinner, followed by baths, bedtime routine, and lights out. I have looked at that day as a failure. I was impatient, discouraged, not really all that kind to my children, and when I went out to play, I didn't have a great time. After about ten minutes I thought, "Wow, it is really cold. I think I am getting frostbite. There isn't anyone else out and I just want to go back in the house!"

And yet, it was Stephanie's favorite childhood memory. THIS was the day she would talk about at my funeral. She didn't know how I felt about the day. She wasn't aware of or didn't remember the mistakes I had made. I made ONE right choice that day next to about 20 wrong choices. But the one right choice: to go out and play, made her day. After the shock of this experience, I asked the rest of my children for their favorite memories. Here is a list of their responses:

"Mom and I sitting by the fire reading books and eating Red Vines."

"Renting *Teenage Mutant Ninja Turtles Part II* and eating pizza as a family."

"Renting a Super Nintendo and Mom playing 'Super Mario Brothers' with us."

"Lying to us about our Christmas presents in order to maximize the surprise factor on Christmas Day."

"Letting me pretend to be a fireman, archaeologist and Ghostbuster all in one day."

"Supporting me at soccer even though she knew none of the rules."

"Oatmeal baths when we had the chickenpox."

"Singing us to sleep with 'You are My Sunshine' and other songs." (Thank you.)

"Being an active partner to help us solve our own problems and teaching us that every problem has a solution."

"Coming to cross country and track meets all over the Dallas/Fort Worth Metroplex."

"Taking me to Pizza Hut to get a cheese pizza just for me." (A *Home Alone* reference, an Anderson family favorite.)

"Walking to Maid Marion park with Winnie (our dog)."

"Pretending not to know about our 'sneak attacks' on the presents early Christmas morning."

"When I was in Little League and had to play a game without my glasses and I was so scared they would hit a ball to me in right field. Sure enough, they did and I could barely see it, but by some miracle, I caught it. You told me afterwards that as soon as you saw the ball fly into the air you had said a little prayer to help me catch it."

"Supporting me in getting my Eagle Scout."

"Buying us nets to catch frogs in the pond."

"Signing me up for nature classes and letting me go exploring afterwards at Sippo Lake with Mark Varner."

"The start of summer break family meeting where we would make lists of all the fun stuff we wanted to do that summer."

"Every time I'd leave to go somewhere, you'd always say the same thing: 'Remember who you are.'"

This list of memories reminds me that it is in the everyday that memories are made. Some of the things they mentioned I hadn't even remembered. Most of the things they mentioned took no planning or arranging on my part. Motherhood cannot be planned and mapped out for success. Sing your songs, make your mistakes, and find the serendipity in each day. If you want to know how you are doing, ask your children, "What is your favorite memory?" Sit back and prepare to be surprised. Note to my children: I would still like it if you all sang my silly songs at my funeral.

CHAPTER FIVE

Loss

"Surely He hath borne our griefs, and carried our sorrows." Isaiah 53:4

*W*ell, that didn't go well," said my daughter through tears the day she went in for a routine prenatal ultrasound. The technician had noticed some sort of abnormality on the scan. Caroline and Blake were told that their son had an Encephalocele birth defect, one so severe that he would not be able to live more than a few minutes out of the womb.

Life was forever changed for my daughter, her husband, and all of our family that day. Dayne Taylor Williams was born a week later, lived moments, and returned to his Father in Heaven. As I reflect on Dayne's birth and death, I am amazed at the many lessons Dayne taught me about loss, healing, life, and God.

1. Dayne taught me that there is no glue.

We often hear the words, "my heart is broken." Although that is not technically what happens, it is how it feels. Loss leaves us with a rip in our heart, painful and raw. I expressed to my daughter that I wished I had some magic glue that could instantly mend her heart. But, in the darkening grip of grief and sorrow, life as Caroline knew it was changed. Her life had shifted. She watched the world carelessly carry on as the pain borne of the realization that she will miss Dayne all of her life tried to swallow her whole. The tear in her heart could not be simply glued back together, reverting it to its original shape, and causing it to look like new. The heart does not heal in this way. Caroline needed a healing balm to fill the chasms, not simply stitching her heart back together, but enlarging it, until one day, she found that she is more now than she was before.

Recognizing that there is no singular path to healing for those who are grieving, and in the absence of "glue," I would like to reflect on three ways we might be able to begin the process of filling in the tears that loss can leave in our hearts.

First, remembering. Remembering gives us strength. The day after Dayne was born, women from Caroline's ward brought us all dinner. I watched with such happiness the joy and love evident in both Caroline and Blake's faces as they recounted the story of Dayne's birth to those wonderful women. They were both glowing with parental pride; they shared the pictures of their sweet boy. I found myself doing the same thing. When people would ask how Caroline and Blake were doing, I would pull out the pictures, eager to share Dayne's profoundly sweet spirit. I had a need and a desire to remember him, to make sure others know that he is my nineteenth grandchild and part of our family.

Remembering helps others. About a year after Dayne died, Caroline had the opportunity to talk with another woman who was going through a similar experience. During the conversation, she realized how far she had come and all she had learned. Caroline was overwhelmed with gratitude to be able to help someone else going through the same thing. The words "I know how you feel" carried weight and comfort. A woman who had walked down the same painful road could help another make her way along the path.

There are many healing ways to remember our loss. For example, one could commemorate a child's birthday with acts of service, or an empty nester could remember what it was like to have a full nest and help other mothers who are still in that season of life. Remembering fun memories and happy times of a child with whom there is conflict can give us hope and strength. As we remember how we got out of bed every day and faced life, we help others do the same. Remembering gives us strength, a healing strength for ourselves and strength to help heal others.

Second, the healing power of service is a soothing balm that fills the heart. Consider the Lord's paradoxical logic in the following statement: "Whosoever will lose his life for my sake shall find it."[10] It is notable to me that Jesus uses the word "lose" in this example. The Savior is teaching that loss is a vital component of our eternal progression to become someone new (and better) than we were before. We are changed as we give ourselves over to the Lord. In return, he helps to heal our loss by finding a new path, a new way. He assures us, "I will not leave you comfortless, I will come to you."[11]

After Dayne was born, a hospice nurse came into the room and lovingly took pictures and made a casting of his sweet, tiny hands and feet. She gave her own time and used her own resources to provide Caroline and Blake with pictures, treasures that will keep their memories of Dayne alive, treasures that will be passed down and shared with others for generations.

The hospice nurse explained that her own daughter had died at age two. She expressed that serving strengthened her; it helped her to remember her child while also enabling her to help in the healing process for Caroline, Blake and countless others as she helps them remember, too.

Third is the healing power of love. The few days between when I first heard Caroline's heartbreaking news and before I could get to her, I felt so helpless. I asked her, "What can I do? What do you need?" She told me she wanted a "mom hug." Caroline and Blake lived in another state at the time, over a thousand miles from Rich and me. I thought, how do I send her "mom hugs" or love for the few days before I could get to her. So I began texting her hearts. Lots of hearts. After I sent the first ones, she asked me, "Did you

---

10 *The Bible: Authorized King James Version.* Oxford University Press, 1998. Matthew 16:25.

11 *The Bible: Authorized King James Version.* Oxford University Press, 1998. John 14:18.

mean to send me that many hearts?" I said "No! I wanted to send you more! I can never send you enough hearts to equal how much I love you and want to be there for you." I thought of the days when my kids were small and a kiss and a hug could heal all wounds. I know that wonderful childhood ritual can't heal the losses of adult life, but I have learned to not underestimate the power of it, either.

Again, the lesson I learned is that there is no glue that mends a broken heart. What might help one does not help the other. Remembrance, service and love as healing balms may not reflect your individual and sometimes lonely path. Even as I watch them help Caroline and Blake, all of this time later, grief still is Caroline and Blake's companion. Regardless of the healing balm that has soothed their hearts, their hearts won't be fully mended until Dayne is once again in their arms.

2. Dayne taught me about the Lord's Joy.

I learned that the Lord's Joy can be found in any circumstance. I am not talking about happiness, the kind that comes from earthly delights like a new couch or day out with friends. I am talking about a Celestial Joy that can only come from God. "The joy we feel has little to do with the circumstances of our lives and everything to do with the focus of our lives. When the focus of our lives is on God's plan of salvation . . . and Jesus Christ and His gospel, we can feel joy regardless of what is happening—or not happening—in our lives. Joy comes from and because of Him. He is the source of all joy."[12] In the Lord's Joy, there is no sorrow, no fear or doubt. Only hope and love.

We had all anticipated Dayne's birth with tears and fears, knowing that with his birth would come his death. But, when he was born, the only thing I could feel was Joy. Joy filled the room as we

---

12 Russell M. Nelson, "Joy and Spiritual Survival," *Ensign*, November 2016.

were invited into his Celestial world. I saw Joy and love reflected in Caroline and Blake's faces as they held their son. I felt Joy for the plan of salvation that allows our families to be bound together eternally. I felt Joy at the love our Heavenly Father and our Savior have for my family and for all of His children.

We felt Dayne's love for his family, for his mother and father, and he felt our love for him. There was Joy as we felt his wonderful, huge spirit. We felt Joy in the understanding that we don't have to wait until we die to know him or feel his influence. Dayne is with us every day, doing his work on the other side of the veil for his family on earth and in heaven.

To revisit the previously mentioned quote from Russell M. Nelson, "When the focus of our lives is on God's plan of salvation . . . we can feel joy regardless of what is happening." Dayne's birth and death were a testimony of the Great Plan of Salvation. Worries about my other children, their choices, and the trials they were presently going through felt lighter, placed in the proper perspective. There was only hope and knowledge that because of the Lord's Atonement, the covenants I keep, and the promises of the Plan of Salvation, everything will be fine. At a time in my life when I was struggling to find hope, hope was the only thing I could feel.

3. Dayne taught me that life is but a brief moment.

"This is our one and only chance at mortal life—here and now. The longer we live, the greater is our realization that it is brief. Opportunities come, and then they are gone. I believe that among the greatest lessons we are to learn in this short sojourn upon the earth are lessons that help us distinguish between what is important and what is not."[13]

---

13 Thomas S. Monson, "Finding Joy in the Journey," *Ensign*, November 2008.
   © By Intellectual Reserve, Inc.

Dayne waited until just the right moment to make his entry into the world. He came at the same time every nurse on the floor was called away to assist Caroline's doctor in an emergency C-section for another patient. Because of that, Dayne was delivered by, and went straight into, his earthly father's hands. He stayed with us for just a moment and then returned to his Father in Heaven. But, what a moment it was. In that moment, Dayne taught us more about the Plan of Salvation than we could ever learn in a lifetime of study. He taught us about the joy that exists in the Lord's presence. He taught us about faith and hope. The Lord had a plan for Dayne as He has a plan for all of us. Dayne had a moment to fulfill his earthly mission before he returned to heaven. He continues to teach us as we ponder and remember that wonderful day. That was his mission in his moment of life. In the eternal perspective, even if we were to live one hundred years, our life only represents a brief moment of our eternal existence.

No one is sent to the earth "just because." Like Dayne, we come here with the Lord's plan for us. Our plan includes trials, hardships, aches and pains. It includes opportunities, responsibilities and blessings. We all have gifts that help others move through their dark days. Often, these gifts (and opportunities to make a difference) develop from our own painful experiences.

I have been wondering about the moment I am spending here on Earth. Am I doing with it what the Lord wants me to do? Are there other things I should be doing? All of us can ask: what will we do, and what does the Lord want us to do with "our moment"?

4. Dayne taught me I control nothing.

Mothers are control freaks. True story. We decide when everyone eats, sleeps, does chores, leaves for school, goes places, comes home from places. We decide what grades and behavior are acceptable. We tell our children what to say and what not to say. We decide when it's time for noise and time for quiet. We control everything. We may be under the impression that by our attempts to control all of this, we can actually control ALL of this, but in reality, that is an illusion. The losses and events in our lives (other than the ones we create by our choices) are not in our control.

At the drop of a dime, the reality that we do not control, cause or prevent anything changes us. We can become uncertain, go spiraling down to a place where we feel because of the loss we are weaker, or we take on guilt that doesn't belong to us. Women who are not able to have children mistakenly think there is something wrong with them, children of divorce quickly feel guilty as if they did something wrong.

I am consistently under the delusion that if I can control the events of life, then I can also control the outcome, so that nothing bad ever happens to my children. As I have watched my "sweet Caroline" go through this time of sorrow and grief, I am struck with the realization that Dayne's death was beyond my control and I find myself wishing I could take on her pain. I would gladly bear it, if it meant she didn't have to. But, as I watch her and Blake let go and trust God and His healing power, I am also watching the miraculous insights, experiences, and blessings they are receiving through their faith and devotion to the Savior. I have come to the realization that if I took the pain, I would also take the blessings. The Lord trusted her and is compensating her for enduring this trial, and I will trust the Lord.

5. Dayne taught me we are all the same.

As a young man, Blake completed two years of missionary service for our church in Africa. It was early in his mission when he attended his first funeral. His missionary companion explained the African tradition of all the men at the funeral helping to fill in the grave while the women sang. His companion said, "It doesn't matter who you are, or how expensive your suit is, you grab a shovel and help fill the grave."

And so, two days after his birth, we buried Dayne in the South African tradition. I watched with great emotion as Blake lay on his stomach, in his suit, and gently placed the small coffin into the ground. And then, while we all sang the hymn "God Be with You Till We Meet Again," all of the men filled in the grave.

We are all the same. We are all God's children. No one is immune from earthly trials and sorrows. But as we slip into the dark shadows of grief, we might say, "If God loved me, He wouldn't allow this to happen. If this doesn't happen to others, He must love them more than me." Our earthly sojourn, our moment of time, is not a test of God's love for us. He has proven His love. Our moment of time is for us to prove ourselves to God. Even in the depths of loss, grief and despair.

No one is outside of God's healing reach. "Surely he hath borne our grief and carried our sorrows."[14] Blessings are not hoarded and parceled out bit by bit according to God's pleasure, but they are given freely and in abundance to all of us if we will lean on Him.

6. Dayne reminded me to "look up."

I like to go to the zoo. Here in Texas, I get to go often during the winter because of our milder temperatures. Even so, there are times when it is a bit chilly. On days like that, I love to sit on a bench (usually across from the zebras) and then look up. I find and move my face towards the sun. The feeling of the sun's rays makes me smile and provides warmth on a cold day. Loss can follow us like a shadow on a chilly afternoon, but as I have watched Caroline grieve, remember, serve, and reach out to help others who are walking her same path, I see those things giving her the strength to be able to seek light and warmth, not from the sun in the sky like I do when I am at the zoo and feeling cold, but from the Son of God, whose

---

14 *The Bible: Authorized King James Version*. Oxford University Press, 1998. Isaiah 5:4.

light brings her healing warmth as she turns her face (full of grief, sorrow and loss) towards Him.

Loss. It doesn't matter your circumstance; loss will be part of your life. There will be hard moments, days, weeks or even years. All women will at times feel loss. It may be loss of a child, the inability to have children, loss of a full nest, or the loss of a child whose choices take him or her away from us. It could be the loss of expected opportunities or dreams when reality and circumstance come crashing in. We experience the loss of a spouse, loss of personal health, loss of parents through death or divorce. Any of these common human experiences can make us feel like we have had more than our share of heartache, pain, and sorrow that threaten to swallow us up. Whatever life has to offer me, no matter the heart-aching loss, I try to remember the things Dayne taught me and not forget the best the Lord has to offer if we just "look up."

CHAPTER SIX

Women Need Women

"When women lock arms, they help each other to accomplish great things. "

I love my friendships. I love the experiences I've had with friends and the strength I've received from all of them. One of my favorite memories is when a few friends of mine decided it would be fun to sew matching dresses for our daughters who were around the same age. We chose a matching pattern and fabric. Everyone came over and we spent the day in my basement sewing all four dresses (including four matching hats). The next Sunday, the girls wore their dresses. They all looked so cute! Every time I look at the pictures we took, it is not just the dresses or the cute girls wearing them that make me smile, it is the memory of friendship and love between friends.

Women need women. Marjorie Hinckley said it best, "We are all in this together. We need each other. Oh, how we need each other. Those of us who are old need you who are young, and hopefully, you who are young need some of us who are old. It's a sociological fact that women need women. We need deep and satisfying and loyal friendships with each other. These friendships are a necessary source of sustenance." She goes on to say that as women, we need to "lock arms" and "renew our faith every day."[15]

Sister Hinckley describes a network of women, all intertwined. We gain power as we help each other through our greatest trials. We celebrate each other. We commiserate with each other. We serve one another, love one another, cry and laugh with one another. We survive because of this great need. Counterintuitively, it's our

---

15 *Glimpses into the Life and Heart of Marjorie Pay Hinckley*, ed. Virginia H. Pearce (Salt Lake City: Deseret Book Company, 1999), 254-255. © By Deseret Book Company. Used with permission.

vulnerabilities that allow us to experience the relieving strength and power of female friendships and service.

Life-defining female bonds often emerge in times of pain and trouble to offer shared strength and perspective. We see this play out in the Old Testament in the story of Ruth's devotion to Naomi when Naomi felt she had nothing more to offer. Ruth's words of assurance created a bond of needed strength and fortitude for both women during a time of trial, anxiety and grief.[16] We see it again in the New Testament, with Elizabeth and Mary's kinship, which was brought on by miraculous pregnancies. The shared experiences of Mary and Elizabeth must have been balm to their souls. There was no other woman who would understand the feelings of Mary's heart more than Elizabeth, and no other woman who would understand Elizabeth more than Mary.[17]

Although these women were of various ages, circumstances and experiences, all four women, through their friendships, were able to each give the other what they needed and, in that process, each woman found her strength. These stories mirror our friendships today. Indeed, we have all had times when it was women who strengthened us in our need, let us rest our weary heads, and helped us see light through some of the darkest parts of our life.

I am thankful for the Ruths in my life, those wonderful women who say just the right thing when it needs to be said.

When I was 15, my parents were going through a divorce; it was a difficult time, and I heard a lot of people say to me that I always looked "so sad." I didn't know what to do with that. Should I not be sad? Was I in trouble for being sad? I didn't know why they said that nor did I know how to process my feelings. Except to state the obvious, no one seemed to be able to help me, which was no help at all.

---

16 *The Bible: Authorized King James Version.* Oxford University Press, 1998. Ruth 1.

17 *The Bible: Authorized King James Version.* Oxford University Press, 1998. Luke 1:39-56.

One day in my church class for young women, my advisor concluded her lesson (I can't remember the subject) by going around the classroom and saying something she liked about each of us. I was uncomfortable. I was scared she would have nothing to say about me, and I was hastily looking at the door and windows trying to make and execute an exit plan before it was my turn. I failed. She turned to me and said without hesitation, "I love your smile. When you smile, the room lights up." It was so simple, at a time when I felt so alone, and in a situation no one understood. When I was surrounded by others who never knew what to say, she was able to say the exact thing I needed to hear at the exact time I needed to hear it. I remember being so surprised that I smiled!

Although this youth leader was older than me, she was my Ruth. With those simple words, she was able to look through my current situation and help me begin removing the weight of sadness. Because she didn't hesitate when she came to me, I recognized a sincere compliment. I needed someone to look through my sadness and see something beautiful. The surprise I felt when I smiled, the realization that I could smile, gave me hope that I wouldn't always be sad. I knew someone understood and it comforted me to know I wasn't alone. From my need to be able to figure a way out of the sadness came solace and hope. I will remember forever the lifeline to happiness she gave me.

I am thankful for the Elizabeths in my life, for the friends who speak with their hearts. When I sent my oldest son on his two-year mission for our church, another woman who had just sent out her youngest came up to me one Sunday. We were different ages; she had an empty nest, and mine was still full. But, as we met each other and looked into each other's eyes, our hearts did the talking. I knew she knew how I felt, and she knew I knew how she felt.

This experience manifested itself again several years later as I attended my grandson's funeral. A friend of mine, whom I had not seen in several years, came to offer support. When I saw her walking down the hill towards the grave, my heart leapt with joy. Her hug and her tears helped give me the ability to get through the rest of that difficult day.

Just as Elizabeth heard Mary calling, these women answered my needs. I am thankful for my friends who know when to call, when to check in, and when to show up on my doorstep with a large, ice-cold beverage (my granddaughter Ellie's word for soda pop).

Women need women. My concern is that in what seems to be a growing climate of comparison and competition, these kinds of friendships and sources of strength that I described may be dwindling. Instead of women building each other up, they become further isolated from the very help and encouragement they need.

Comparison and competition are evil twins. Do not give these sisters an inch. They are quick and deadly. With every comparison, every failed attempt to keep up with the perceived "perfect mothers," or have our lives and homes reflect our latest Pinterest boards, they convince us that our worries are many and solutions are few. Comparison tells us in one ear that we are not good enough. She encourages us to compare our life against others instead of appreciating and nurturing who we are. In the other ear, competition tells us we have to try harder as she points out our friends on Facebook and other social media platforms announcing their trips, awards, perfect homes, and perfect children. Both sisters work hard creating within us dissatisfaction with our life and ourselves. These sisters try to tell us that we are on our own. We don't have to be. We all can do things others cannot. But together, if we turn our backs on comparison and competition and combine our talents and gifts, we become a powerful force for good.

We gain strength from personal friendships. In addition, an entire group of women needing women can bring power to our families, our communities, and ourselves. Marjorie Hinckley says that "as women we need to . . . lock arms" and "renew our faith every day." There is something wonderful that happens when women come together and work for a common cause. We all need this kind of association.

When I think of an example of what can happen when women "lock arms," I am drawn to the story of the "stripling warriors," found in The Book of Mormon.[18] Traditionally, this story centers on the 2,000 sons of the people of Ammon. My thoughts on this story, however, center on the Ammonite women who taught and influenced those young boys throughout their lives. These young men had no experience with war and yet they were brave in the face of a war-hardened enemy. They were obedient and respectful. They relied on and remembered their God. The unanimous faith of all the stripling warriors speaks to the strength of a community of women who had instilled a knowledge of their faith deep into the young men's souls. I am sure that family and friends all had a part in teaching and raising these young men, but the scriptures tell us that it was the promises and faith of their mothers they took into battle.

I picture this group of women as a community of dear friends. I imagine they knew each other, and together, lived in a way that their lives were a reflection of their testimonies, the oaths they made, and the price they paid to keep their promises to God.

Just imagine the power of all of those mothers' prayers being offered each day for those brave young men. The effects of these prayers are evident in the fact that although they were bruised and battered, they all came home.

None of us lives in a community with this kind of unusual history, but I believe the women of Ammon were a society of women not entirely unlike our own. Just like in our day, the mothers of

18 The Book of Mormon. Salt Lake City: The Church of Jesus Christ of Latter-day Saints, 2013. Alma 56-58.

the two thousand young men, and other women living in the land of Jershon, would have experienced various life circumstances. Some were older, some younger. Some were friends and sisters of the warriors; some women were married, some were not. Some had children, some did not. There would have been widows who had relied on their sons or other young men for help and support. There would have been women dealing with illness, or an illness of a child or husband. In the time these boys were gone, other life events must have occurred. Babies were born, people died; no matter how great their faith in the outcome of their sons' service, there had to be days when they were worried—days when their hearts ached—missing their sons.

What a happy reunion and sight to behold that must have been when all the young men returned. In my mind's eye, I can see these women—who had helped and served and loved each other and prayed for every young man—gathered with their families as their sons returned. I can see each young man walking through the gates and someone calling out his name: "Here he is!" they would cry, making sure he found his way to his family. When I think of this wonderful scene, I see all of the women staying at the gate until the last son came through. And after being hugged by their mother and families, the young men are embraced by all the women there. And in each woman's prayers to God thanking Him for the safe return of her son(s), she includes her gratitude for the return of all.

These strong women would not have left each other alone to struggle or feel sad. Meals and other acts of service would have been organized for the sisters who were ill. Sons, daughters, and fathers still at home would have filled in for those who needed help. Like us, they needed each other, hugged, laughed, and cried with each other. They "locked arms" and together "renewed their faith every day."

When women lock arms like the mothers of Ammon did, the loads they carry can seem smaller and the days will seem to pass more quickly. Using our gifts and talents together will assist us in accomplishing great things.

When I was younger, I played the flute and participated in the school orchestra. I found myself somewhat frustrated during practice. I loved playing what I call the "fun parts," where in any given piece of music the flute had many notes to play and seemed to be leading. But, there were other parts I found boring. These included measures my flute would be at rest or had very few notes for me to play. It was tempting to concentrate my practice on the fun sections and leave the boring ones unpracticed. But, when the orchestra played as one, I saw how each measure I played fit in; every instrument had an important role in the sound of the overall song.

When my flute was at rest, other instruments would come in and shine. While I was playing one or two notes per measure, others would fill in with beautiful companion notes. When it was the flute's time to play the lead, I appreciated the other instruments playing their supporting notes. None of us playing our instruments by ourselves would have sounded as good—we all needed each other. We needed the different sounds the various instruments made. This combination of notes, instruments, and skill levels combined to create a strong, beautiful, and harmonious song.

Naomi, Ruth, Mary, Elizabeth, and the women of Ammon all played their parts. We can hear their beautiful songs and see the strength coming from their need for each other—for friendship, for working toward a cause, and for understanding and comfort. We and they are part of this great symphony of women in the world. Like the various measures my flute played, there will be times we will be at rest while others shine. Sometimes we will play a strong, supporting role to our companions. Sometimes we will have a flurry of activity of our own. I know there will be times when it will be hard to see what impact we are making from our view of real life (like when I practiced the flute), and we may not be able to hear how the beautiful music will sound. We may not understand our part in the song, or feel we have much to contribute. But, if we need and strengthen one another in faith, adding our unique voice to the song, we will hear the music, our children will hear it, and we will raise up generations of women who will continue to sing.

CHAPTER SEVEN

No Initials After My Name

"Confidence is going after Moby Dick in a rowboat
and taking the tartar sauce with you."
—Zig Ziglar

I have a long-running joke with my kids. Sometimes the kids would see me do something they had no idea I knew how to do. One example would be the time the boys were playing basketball on our driveway and I stole the ball, dribbled a couple of times and shot the ball at the basket. (It's not important to know whether or not I scored.) A look of befuddlement came across their faces, and with more skepticism than the situation warranted, they asked me, "Do you know how to play basketball?" Kids are always shocked to find their parents know anything more than just the basics of life. My answer to this and other questions of this type were always the same: "Yes, I know how to play basketball. I could have been a professional basketball player, but I gave it up to be a mother." (I'm 5 foot, 3 and 3/4 inches, so you can assume this was a fictitious answer.) I might have fooled them the first few times I used that, but they quickly caught on and over the years, the joke has become part of our family. I have claimed to be an expert in many areas: doctor, chef, lawyer, you name it. Even now, the kids all enjoy asking me these same kinds of questions and then saying, "Wait, I know: you could have been a professional, but you gave it up to be a mother." I tell them they are correct and accept their accolades for my selflessness.

All kidding aside though, unlike some of the professions I claimed to have had, I have no initials or titles after my name. There isn't a degree in motherhood. There is no school for mothering; there is no five-year star or ten-year star we earn. There are no levels of certification we have to attain, or any document we can hang up on our walls showing our qualifications. We start this venture with limited skills and knowledge, and the only institute of motherhood is the "University of Do Your Best," while the curriculum is "learn as you go." Because of this, confidence becomes an important attribute to develop. Also because of this, confidence can be elusive—it can come and go depending on how we judge the events or outcome of every day.

Zig Ziglar said, "Confidence is going after Moby Dick in a rowboat and taking the tartar sauce with you."[19] What a great representation of motherhood! In this scenario, I like to think that the rowboat represents not only how we start each day, but our willingness to engage in each day. And *Moby Dick*—the great story of unpredictable adventure where Captain Ahab seeks the great whale with the single-minded goal of slaying it—is a fitting metaphor for us. We, too, go out into the unknown of each new day with a lofty goal. Spoiler alert: Captain Ahab does not succeed in slaying the great white whale. Unlike the infamous captain however, we *can* find success. But it is not Captain Ahab I want to concentrate on in this analogy. It is the tartar sauce. In this quote, tartar sauce symbolizes the confidence mothers must take into each day to overcome all odds and do things they have never done before. It symbolizes a trust in our abilities and innate resources to slay the great white whale and navigate the unpredictable waters of motherhood.

As inspiring of a picture as Mr. Ziglar's quote paints, we might ask, "How do we develop confidence in tasks and responsibilities we've never had before?" If we were going to put together a jar of tartar sauce (or a jar of confidence), what are some of the ingredients we will need in that jar?

First ingredient: Make a plan.

When children are born, you could say that by definition, they are selfish; life revolves around them. They cry when they are hungry or tired or hurt. When they are little and don't yet know how to

---

19 Zig Ziglar, "Ziglar.com," Ziglar, 2018. Used with permission.

use their words, we run around trying to figure out what they need. As they mature, we teach them how to become selfless, i.e., we teach them to think less about themselves and be more aware of others and the world around them. We teach them how to use their words when they want something and how to share. Instead of running around meeting every need, we teach them how to cope with boredom and unhappiness and how to solve their own problems. We teach them to think of and serve others. We teach them to think of themselves as part of a community to which they can contribute. This very process of moving from selfish to selfless is hard. Think of how little we enjoy the process of change (a.k.a., "growth opportunities"), and yet we ask our children to do it on a daily basis as they are continually taught, stretched, and corrected. Can we really be surprised if this process is met with some resistance and is a bit bumpy at times?

Helping our children through their childhood requires confidence that what we are trying to teach outweighs any negative reaction to the teaching. How many times do we give children a consequence for a wrong choice and ask ourselves, "Is this worth it? Do I really want to stick to my guns? Is it easier to let them have their way?" It takes great confidence to be consistent and keep our resolve. It also requires a plan.

When Rich and I were young parents with small children, we began having questions regarding the best way to teach and discipline our children. We asked many of our friends as well as seasoned parents. We got a variety of answers. They ranged all the way from, "Consult this or that child psychology book and read the risk analysis of each parental action," to, "Show them who is in charge and spank them for everything."

As we discussed the various advice, the very different ways we were raised, and what was really important to us, we came to the realization that parenting had to begin, above all else, with love for our children. We put together a plan that reflected that love and included various theories from things we had read, our own ideas, ideas from others, prayerful discernment, understanding of our talents, and our moral code. We discussed the ways we would execute our plan. This is the how of parenting—how do we get them from point A to point B? This conversation, which started when we first began our family, continues today. As more children came into our family, we realized that one size does not fit all and even though our values and overall plans and goals for our family didn't change, we learned to have enough confidence to adapt and change "the plan" according to the individuality, situation and ages of our children.

When my older children were younger, and before the concept of a "time out" became popular, it was "go to your room." When someone wasn't playing nice with others or throwing a fit or just needed some away time, I would have them go spend some time in their room. This was fairly successful for the older siblings, but when Caroline and Michael came along, "going to their room" didn't work. I tried the "time out" technique and it didn't work either.

They both had the same issues, but required different solutions.

Caroline

I would tell Caroline she needed some "time out" and have her go to another room or sit in a chair, but I couldn't get her to stay there without it becoming a bigger fight than what she had been sent to "time out" for.

One day, Caroline was doing something she shouldn't and I thought, "What will I do? What will work?" What bothered Caroline about being sent to her room and time out was that she took being sent away personally. She didn't correlate a wrong choice with the need for some time to calm down and think about things. She internalized this consequence with the feeling that she was no longer wanted by the group. So, on this particular occasion, I had the thought to tell her she was "on a spot." She immediately stopped what she was doing and asked, "Where is the spot?"

"Where you are standing," I replied.

I explained: she could stay with us, but couldn't move from the spot. Oh my, she was not happy. "I don't want to be on a spot," she would say. But it worked. She didn't move. The next time she was making some wrong choices I said, "if you do THAT again, you will be on a spot." The spot was something she tried to avoid like the plague. The warning of "The Spot" was often all that was needed. One day, the warning was ignored and she found herself once more on the dreaded SPOT. She stood or sat (either was fine) there and thought. Finally, she thought she had found the loophole in my newly-designed consequence. Caroline said, "I am not staying on The Spot, see? I am running around." I told her the spot went wherever she went. Again, she was NOT happy. To this day, as an adult I will tease her and tell her I am putting her on a spot and she still looks at me as if to say, "NO, NOT THE SPOT!"

Michael

Michael also did not like going to his room. (And to be honest, as child number seven, he sometimes got forgotten there as the business of the house took over.) Time outs with him resulted in the same fight I had had with Caroline. So, one day I told him if he didn't stop doing what he was doing, he would be put on a spot. He could not have cared less. He wouldn't stay put and when he found out the spot would move with him; he saw the flaw Caroline never figured out—that the spot only had power insofar as you gave it power. Basically, he had a ticket to continue doing what he was doing with or without a spot so long as he didn't care he was on one.

One day, he was at a friend's house and I told him it was time to go. He wouldn't come and he kept playing. Finally, out of desperation, I told him he was making a wrong choice. He flew into a panic, ran up to me, put on his coat and was at the door. Very interesting, I thought. I already knew Michael would do anything for a song. I had a song for picking up toys, helping, getting up, going to bed, etc. After the revelation that Michael did not like making wrong choices, I made up what is known in our family as "The Wrong Choice/Right Choice Song." All I had to do was start singing, "Michael's making a wrong choice, wrong choice, wrong choice . . .," and he would correct what he was doing and insist I sing the right choice song, which was, "Michael's making a right choice, right choice, right choice . . ."

Two different children, both with the same challenge. One way didn't work for both of them. Confidence gives us the strength needed to come up with out-of-the-box solutions and help us parent our children individually according to who they are. Do you always see daily results? No. Confidence doesn't guarantee that each day's challenges will be surmounted. Confidence is knowing you did your best using tools that you trust. It enables us to get up every morning, grab that jar of confidence and jump back into the rowboat.

Second ingredient: Give yourself some time.

I never bought Band-Aids. Never. Well, every once in a while, I did, and it only made me more determined to never buy Band-Aids again. You know the drill: you buy Band-Aids and EVERYTHING becomes a life-threatening injury. Every scratch becomes a DEFCON 1 "blood pouring out of my body" thing, and before you know it, the box of Band-Aids is gone.

I didn't always have a No Band-Aid Policy. I have seven children and for the first few years, everything required a Band-Aid, doctor visit or trip to the emergency room.

We all remember our reaction when our first child fell down and got hurt the first time. We almost passed out when we saw our child's first drop of blood. We would wash it, call the doctor and our mother. Statements were taken from all those who were present: what did you see? How did this happen? Band-Aids are applied; kisses, hugs and ice cream are generously given. Plans for a mobile cage that goes around your child are drawn up.

But, after time and more children come around, you learn that not everything needs a Band-Aid. My reaction of treating all medical events as emergencies declined over time.

The red flag for going to the emergency room went from "everything" to being reserved only for sticks or bones protruding out of the skin, or an arm that was in an odd position accompanied by a very white-faced child. Things that did not bring up the red flag may have included, but were not limited to, times when Michael fell down the stairs (which, I am sad to say, he did on a regular basis for the first 10 years of his life). On occasion, he would hit the corner of a stair and cut his head. Let me explain, were there times it looked like it needed stitches? Probably. But for the most part, I pushed it together and put a butterfly type Band-Aid over the cut. (Yes, I went to the store and bought some).

While at first, everything was an emergency, over the years, I learned to tell the exact temperature of a child by touching their stomach. I knew which kind of cough would go away and which kind needed a doctor's attention. I knew that when Michael threw up without any other symptoms, he had strep throat. I learned the hard way that when a child (Stephanie) had a pain in between their shoulder blades, she might have pneumonia. Did this more relaxed approach to sickness, scrapes and injuries ever come back to haunt me? Have I ever treated something or dismissed symptoms I should have left to the professionals? My children would tell you that I did. Remember, I didn't have Dr. Google; I was on my own. However, my confidence outweighed the worry and I found that the mistakes were part of the learning process. And although I have Band-Aids on hand for my cute grandchildren, who can have them anytime, the point is, once we get a little experience behind us, we start to ease up on a few things and find that common sense plus a little less panic is usually what is needed. It is in this process that from both our successes and failures we learn, and are able to replace worries with confidence. An assurance in our abilities for any given area of motherhood increases.

Third ingredient: Trust in the long game.

Without confidence in the long game, we are sometimes unsure of how to parent. The idea that our child's faults or missteps spring from our personal failings causes us to mistake our child's immediate reaction for the long term results of our discipline. For instance, if we send our child to their room because they are having a temper tantrum, and they yell, "I hate you forever," we worry that because of our discipline we have caused our child to "hate" us, and that this will be a permanent situation. These kinds of worries can take away confidence and subsequently, our ability to teach our children diminishes. When we have confidence in the long game, we realize that once the fit is over, so is the "hate," and we can set aside our worries and stay the course.

Without confidence in the long game, we could become impatient with the teaching process, and with our children and their ability to learn. "How many times must I tell you?" is a common parental phrase. Wouldn't it be great if our children quickly and permanently changed their behavior every time we corrected them? We don't learn that fast and neither do our children. They need time and experience to define their childhoods and shape their characters.

We need the long game to teach our children many important principles, both spiritual and temporal, as we take them from selfish to selfless. This process needs time and experiences that come from being part of a family: by doing chores, managing money, being kind to one another, and having fun together. Time is needed to build strong family bonds and make lasting memories as we work together to serve others, pray together, support and encourage each other in our individual and family endeavors. Life lessons take time, including learning how to use and choose their words when they are angry, and how to better channel their anger into productive solutions.

For me, one of the things that gave me anxiety was when my kids threatened to run away from home. For some reason, this was my kids' go-to strategy when things did not go their way. It would have been so easy to acquiesce to their demands when the rhetoric got that heated. But, nothing would have been accomplished or learned. So, one day I announced a new family rule. I declared that if you left our home for any reason not on the "approved" list: college, mission, over 18 and working, marriage, etc., you must leave our family in the same condition you came into it: naked. On several occasions and by several of my children, this rule was tested. One day, Daniel (around age 8 or 9) decided, in a whirlwind of anger directed at me, that it was his turn to leave the nest. He declared his intent to run away. I said, "fine, take off your clothes first." Completely stifled, baffled and in disbelief over the cruelty of this rule he said, "MOM, you cannot be serious." I told him, very calmly I might add, that I was, and reminded him about my run away naked rule. Well, he was mad. He realized striking out on his own and making his way in the world would be much trickier without clothes. Defeated but still angry, he said, "I am so mad at you. I will never be through being mad at you. Even when I am 16, I will still be mad at you!" He didn't run away. He turned sixteen and we were fine.

Have the confidence to "stay the course" and believe that the positive things you do with and for your children: teaching, nurturing, listening, and playing with them, outweigh any mistakes made or their angry reactions to "tough love" moments. And you will see, over time, the results of the long game you trusted.

Fourth ingredient: Have confidence in your relationship with God.

For mothers, the day starts around dawn and ends just a few hours before the next dawn, when you can finally sleep. Amid that hustle and bustle, it is easy to neglect the things we should do to build a real, genuine, and personal relationship with the Savior.

"Having such a relationship [with the Savior] can unchain the divinity within us, and nothing can make a greater difference in our lives as we come to know and understand our divine relationship with God."[20] Having this kind of spiritual strength will increase our ability to lay our worries aside and hear the whisperings of the Spirit on behalf of our children. Having this kind of spiritual strength gives us confidence in our abilities to navigate the storms and choppy waters of life. From the very smallest of concerns to the biggest, we can have confidence in the Savior's help.

When Melanie was about two, her Uncle Ryan, who is three weeks older than she is (yes, uncle), was spending the night. We had two beds in Melanie's room. Even though they were identical, there was a bed that was identified as Melanie's bed. Earlier that day, Ryan had taken a nap on Melanie's bed and during the nap, he had wet through his diapers and the mattress. Although the sheets and blanket had been washed, when it was time for bed, the mattress was still wet. Both Melanie and Ryan often slept in the same bed, so that night we put the two children into the other bed together. Ryan settled right down and Melanie started to scream. There was no consoling her, no matter what we tried. Finally, Rich and I said a prayer to help us understand what was making Melanie so upset. "It's the bed," was the clear answer. Because Melanie never really consistently slept in "her bed" when Ryan was over, we had never thought she might be upset with the sleeping arrangements. But the Lord knew. So, we turned over Melanie's wet mattress to the dry side, put on the linens and transferred her to her bed. Melanie turned over, was quiet and went to sleep.

Fifth ingredient: Have confidence in the power of our divine love for our children.

Maternal love is a powerful driving force. It is what motivates us to be present in our children's lives, show up for recitals, games

---

20 James E. Faust, "A Personal Relationship with The Savior," *Ensign*, November 1976. © By Intellectual Reserve, Inc.

and other activities and ceremonies. Because we love them, we are interested in what they are interested in and encourage and support the development of their talents and gifts. Our love for our children gives us strength for the hard parts of motherhood, like walking the hallways of our homes until they get home at night, sitting by a hospital bed, or fiercely loving them regardless of the choices they are making. It gives us the strength and wisdom to listen to their problems and concerns. It is from our love that we send up powerful mothers' prayers to our Heavenly Father on their behalf. Boyd K. Packer said, "There are few things more powerful than the faithful prayers of a righteous mother."[21]

When my son, William, turned 19, he chose to serve a two-year proselyting mission. He was assigned to serve in the Guam/Micronesia Mission. The mission home and office were in Guam, but William's mission covered a number of islands. Many of these islands were separated by hundreds of miles of ocean. He spent his first year on the island of Chuuk and most of his second year on the island of Ebeye. Communication between the mission president on Guam and the missionaries scattered across the ocean consisted of regular phone calls to make sure they were ok and periodic visits from the mission president or his counselors and their wives. Communication home was made through letters, the kind on actual paper that come in your postbox, not inbox. Because of the location, mail took around a week to a week-and-a-half to get from the islands to us in Texas and about the same time going back.

When William was transferred to Ebeye that second year, we learned that the island was made up of volcanic rock, was about half a mile long and 200 yards across. The conditions were quite primitive, but William talked in every letter about his love for the people and their generous and giving hearts.

---

21 Boyd K. Packer, "These Things I Know," *Ensign*, May 2013. © By Intellectual Reserve, Inc.

After Will had been on Ebeye about nine months, I received a memorable letter. William explained that he was very ill and had been for some time. He wasn't sure what was wrong but believed it was something to do with the water.

Ebeye is about 1500 or so miles from the mission home in Guam. Because letters take so long, what had been current news when it was written was now another week past. I am usually very calm in emergencies and take a pretty practical approach to life. I was used to William telling us about his living conditions: they had a cholera outbreak the previous Christmas. But when I read that letter, I knew deep in my soul that William needed help. He needed to get off that island. He needed medical care, better nutrition, and he needed it now. I thought about what to do and decided I would pray. I told Heavenly Father about the letter. I told Him what I thought William needed and I that wanted William off the Island, *now*.

I have never tried to figure out the exact timing of the subsequent events. I do know that it was very soon, within days of my prayer, that the mission president and his wife made their visit to Ebeye. William did inform them he had been sick, but thought he would be ok. The mission president agreed and told Will they would keep him and his companion there. After the president and his wife returned home, she said to her husband that she felt like William needed to be transferred off Ebeye right away. And so he was. He was transferred to the island of Kwajalein, where there was better water, food and medical care. William served there until the end of his mission. When I read the letter explaining these events, he had been safely on the island for over a week and his health was improving. My soul was settled and I offered a heartfelt prayer of gratitude. It was in that moment that I realized the power a mother's prayer wields. To this day, the family talks about the time Mom prayed William off an island. We all have the power in our prayers to pray our children off islands. Not all answers are as immediate, but do not doubt or underestimate the power behind a prayer offered by a mother, and backed with divine love for her children.

In discussing Ziglar's quote about confidence, I have centered in on the jar of tartar sauce as a symbol for confidence. I outlined some of the ingredients I think would be important to put in our jar, but we have not discussed the jar itself. Without the jar to hold the tartar sauce, it would be a mess every time we got into the boat. The same applies to our ingredients. What holds together all those ingredients so that we can best the challenges of our days?

In the movie *The Wizard of Oz*, Dorothy learned that in the end, the power to return home came from her. At a time when Dorothy felt like she was helpless, and with the early exit of the Wizard, she thought she couldn't possibly achieve her goal of returning home to her loved ones. Dorothy turned to Glinda and pleaded for help to get home. Glinda tells her that she no longer needs any help and explains that she has had the power all along to get herself back to Kansas. Dorothy doesn't understand what Glinda means. The Scarecrow jumps in and asks Glinda why she hadn't told Dorothy that before, to which Glinda responds that she wouldn't have believed her. It was something Dorothy had to learn for herself.[22]

This is true for us. The power to believe and have confidence has to come from inside of us. To hold on to the ingredients of confidence, we must choose to believe and have the confidence in our capacity to love and serve, learn and grow. This includes a belief that we are strong, talented, gifted women. It is a belief that what we are doing, regardless of any evidence to the contrary, makes a difference. It is a belief and conviction that doing our best is all that our children ask of us. It is faith in God and His plan, that there is purpose in what we do, that there is divine help.

---

22 Victor Fleming, George Cukor, and Mervyn LeRoy, *The Wizard of Oz*. (1939; Hollywood: Metro Goldwyn Mayer), Film.

Please don't tell my children, but I was never, nor will I ever be a professional basketball player, chef, lawyer, doctor or any of those other things I mentioned. I didn't give up anything like that to be a mother. Neither would I give up being a mother for anything else.

CHAPTER EIGHT

The Power of Chores

"What do you mean my room isn't clean?"

*I*f you were to look up the word "chore," you'd find many forms of the same definition: "Chores are tasks that are viewed as boring or unpleasant." According to my children, chores have a different definition: A way to torture your kids and make them do all of the work. In my family, assigning chores actually became a chore for me! Every time I asked my children to complete a task, it became an argument and the actual completion of the task was delayed as long as possible. My children, much like all of yours, have done some inventive things to get out of chores. Their tactics were relentless and creative.

Top five most common chore-avoidance tactics:

1. "I have to go to the bathroom." Translation: And stay in the restroom until the chores were done.
2. "I don't know how to do this." Translation: I am going to mess this up so badly that mom will never ask me to do it again.
3. "I'm done!" Translation: The job was actually only halfway done, in the hopes that I would not notice what they didn't finish.
4. Sloth. This one is my favorite. (Hopefully my sarcasm can be intuited from the written word). Translation: Work so slowly that they were hardly moving. Their legs wouldn't work, their arms were tired, and they "didn't feel good."
5. "I always have the most chores." Translation: They would list all of the reasons why they were picked on and tortured more than their siblings who, they like to point out, were never asked to do anything.

When those arguments didn't work, they would bring out their second line of defense, peer pressure: "None of my other friends have to do chores." My answer to that "logical" argument was usually an equally "logical" response: "I'm sad your friends' parents don't love them as much as we love you." Finally, the desperation would set in: "I'm NEVER going to make MY kids do chores." (Ok.); "How come the baby doesn't have to do chores?!" (Yes, that's a real quote.); "It's my room, I should be able to keep it how I want" (personal favorite). I am sure you can fill in some of your own.

It does not start out this way; when children are young, they want to help. At three or four years old, Stephanie would ask to do dishes. I would fill up the sink with warm, soapy water, add dishes, and hand her a dishrag. She would stand on a chair, washing and rinsing the dishes, only to put them back into the soapy water and begin the process over. As long as I didn't mind wet counter-tops and some water on the floor (I didn't), she would be happy for hours. However, by the time children are older, the joy of helping has long since faded and they would rather be doing anything else than what they have been asked to do.

"Why do we have to do chores?" I would bet this is one of the most commonly asked questions in all of childhood. It's a good one. As mothers, we may ask: "Why do we add this aggravation to our already stressful days?"

Every spring break, while every other child in the world was allowed to play and do whatever they wanted (I know this because my children told me.), I would engage my children in spring clean-ing. We all worked together. Each day had a new cleaning goal and after we were done, we would do something fun: pizza delivered, movie with treats, etc. There were days the "fun" was lost on my children, and they would solely concentrate on the "unfair" amount of work they were asked to do.

One particular day, we were cleaning the kitchen. Kitchen day was the longest and required the most detailed cleaning. Eric's last job was to clean the fridge. I have to point out that spring cleaning the kitchen did involve some creative tools. I've been known to have my children cover butter knives with washcloths to get the dirt out of small crevices. When that didn't work, I would hand them toothpicks. While I thought this was genius, none of my children shared this opinion. By the end of the day, having to use a knife in this way to clean all of the dirt out of the folds of the weather stripping around the door of the fridge, Eric reached his breaking point. I got the "Why do I have to do this?" question. After I told him it was part of learning how to clean a refrigerator, Eric turned to me and asked, "Mom, why do I need to know how to clean a refrigerator?" I answered, "So that when you get married and know how to keep a fridge clean, your wife will love me." Eric was not amused and to tell the truth, I came up with the answer on the fly. (For the record, Anna, Eric's wife, has expressed gratitude that Eric was taught how to work and clean a house, including the fridge.)

As good of an answer as that was, that was not the reason my children were "asked" to do chores. That alone would not have been enough for me to stay firm and consistent amidst all of their complaints. The answer to "why children should do chores" had to be good and strong, strong enough that I would stand by my belief in the face of any excuse, objection, or tirade.

I came to this understanding one winter at a Relief Society Women's Conference while living in Northeast Ohio. The speaker was home management and family living expert and author, Daryl Hoole. She gave a wonderful talk; it was so encouraging and inspiring. When the subject of chores came up, she said it was her belief that if mothers (parents) taught their children to be responsible for their room and one other room in the house, they would develop the skills they needed to succeed as an adult.

The truth of that statement pierced my soul and by the time she was through speaking, I knew that through the power of chores and the process of learning how to work, my children could grow up to "rule the world." Bold words, I know, but this became my mantra and my purpose. I came home from the conference with a better understanding of the teaching opportunities and the developmental potential of chores. Even though the older ones were already doing chores, it was with this renewed purpose and deeper understanding that, over the years, I was better able to field the complaints, stick with it until they did things right and not back down when they tried (often at the top of their lungs) to convince me my life would be easier if I would just let them off the hook.

I have spent years "torturing" my children based on my belief in Daryl Hoole's message. As a result, I feel some pressure to provide proof that what I believed is true. While writing this chapter, I conducted some research. I found a few studies and a couple of books by experts who cited that the physical actions of work helped develop a child's brain, increased learning, and played a vital role in their development. All of this is good, but it didn't answer the question: do chores have the power to teach our children how to "rule the world?" A thought went through my head: I may not have initials after my name, but I did just fairly recently complete a 32-year observational study on child-rearing. All I had to do was collect, compile and evaluate the results. I asked my children if they could tell me something they learned from doing chores that helps them in their adult life. In other words, are they now ruling THEIR worlds?

Melanie's childhood tactic of choice

Melanie talked about the "I am done" attitude she carried with her as she worked on her chores. When presented with her finished product, we would tell her what she had left to do and then add, "It is a waste of time (and actually takes longer) to do a job halfway."

Adult application: Melanie said, "The work ethic I have today is because of this ideal. When I am faced with a task or job, I figure I might as well dig in and do the job right the first time. Otherwise, it will take me twice as long having to come back and do it right."

William's childhood tactic of choice

William remembered combining "it's too hard" with the "I don't know how to do it" excuse. He was asked to wash the dishes (back before we had a dishwasher) and when it came time to clean the big stuff, all the pots and pans would get "soaked" in soapy water because "they're too hard to scrub." When given instructions on how to actually scrub the pans, he came back with the excuse, "I am not good at scrubbing pans." William said that he remembers those excuses being met with the "Well, there is no time like the present to learn" attitude on my part, and my insisting he keep trying until the job was done correctly.

Adult application: William went to graduate school while holding down a full-time job, a full-time internship, and busy jobs in the church. Not to mention, he was a husband and a father to three children. There were days when he thought, "This is just too hard," and times when he struggled with classes in his program that he felt he wasn't "good at." William said, "I would take the lesson I learned growing up to heart. Just because something is hard or challenging isn't an excuse. It doesn't get you out of doing it. Just because you aren't good at it doesn't mean you get to quit." So, he would solve his problem. He would hire tutors to help him learn and keep going until he finished.

Stephanie's childhood tactic of choice

We ask our children to learn, stretch, and grow. Individual chores and jobs help them do that. They learn that they can accomplish things they didn't think possible. Stephanie talked about some of the hard things she was asked to do and how she felt when they were done.

Adult application: Stephanie said, "I learned and appreciated that you could trust me to do hard things. You knew you could count on me." Now as a mother herself, when life becomes hard, she remembers that I believe in her and her abilities, and this gives her the courage she needs to face her challenges. She said, "I have done hard things before and can do hard things now."

Eric's childhood tactic of choice

Eric said that he remembers being taught the importance of details. When he was assigned a chore, such as cleaning out the fridge, it was important that all of the individual tasks be accomplished before the job was considered complete. For example, the kitchen wasn't cleaned when the dishes were done, nor was your room finished just because you made your bed.

Adult application: Eric teaches high school and says that this attention to detail, and understanding that doing a good job includes more than one task, has helped him develop the skill of remembering and putting weight into the details of his job. He strives to enhance his lessons by finding additional details and insights that might be interesting to his students. This allows for more meaningful discussions than if he had done the bare minimum.

Daniel's childhood tactic of choice

Our family lived in Indiana for about eight years. During that time, we lived in a house with a large, finished basement. Every once in a while (actually more than once and more than a while), it would need a team clean and I would have the kids work together. While they were cleaning, I would periodically go downstairs and check their progress. I would look around, tell them it was looking great but there were other things to do and point out what the next steps should be. The basement was large and it took about four or five passes until the "all done, it looks great" signal was given.

Adult application: Daniel recalled cleaning the basement and said that, as an adult, this process is replicated at his job. He will take a project he is working on and give periodic updates to his boss, who will say something like, "It's a great start, but there is more to do," give him suggestions of what to do next or what else to look at. Sometimes, it takes a few passes before he gets the ok. He said, "Other people at work come out of a meeting like that so upset. They will feel unappreciated for what they have done, or that their boss hates their work. Because I am familiar with this process, I don't take it personally. I trust that the back and forth ultimately leads to the best outcome."

Caroline's childhood tactic of choice

She said, "You always told me that a job worth doing was a job worth doing well." She also remembered doing family work projects, like raking leaves or cleaning the garage. Caroline (and all the children) would ask, "When will we be done?" She remembers Rich saying, "We'll work until the job is done."

Adult application: Caroline has adopted those sayings into her adult life and when working on a project, she and her husband, Blake, say those things to each other to keep them going until they are done. Both of these sentiments are included in their "family constitution."

Michael's childhood tactic of choice

When we moved to Texas, our backyard did not have any landscaped beds, just grass. Because of this, we decided to make some raised beds. Michael and Rich worked out in the yard together. He said that he saw his dad work hard and take pride in a job well done. They worked together laying the bricks around the beds then laying down the dirt, planting, and mulching. He caught his dad's enthusiasm and it became important to him to do a good job. When they were done, he was so pleased to see how good the beds looked and this became one of his favorite memories with his dad.

Adult application: Michael said that when he has a big project for school or work, he remembers how it felt to take pride in his work, take his time, and do his best.

I shouldn't have been, but I was genuinely surprised all seven of my children quickly identified lessons and practical applications that were learned while being given age-appropriate responsibilities as children. Daryl Hoole taught that in the overall picture of things, helping our children be successful in life comes from teaching our children to do for themselves. I believed this to be true when I heard her express this sentiment all those years ago, and I believe it to be true now.

The above lists include very practical applications to their individual chores. But, the power of chores does not stop there. By giving children responsibilities, you can help teach your children about themselves.

Children spend much of their young lives trying to figure out "who they are." They try on different personas, watch for reactions from family and their peers, gauge that reaction and either keep on or change their behavior. Sometimes they need a little help with the "moving on" part.

When Eric was in middle school, I had asked him to put something away. After about the third or fourth time reminding him to do it, he said to me, "Mom, when are you going to just accept that I am lazy?" I did not react to that specific comment but told him to get up and finish his job. But I thought a lot about it later. Now, Eric isn't and wasn't lazy; he was a 14-year-old with an attitude. I came to the conclusion that I would help Eric learn the hard truth: he was not lazy.

This comment was said about a week before the end of the school year. I bided my time and on the first day of summer vacation, I asked him if he would please help me pull down some wallpaper in the front entry hallway. He did. We worked together and when we were finished, I asked him to help me tear some wallpaper down in the kitchen. He did. We worked together and when we were finished,

I asked him to help me put up new wallpaper in the hallway. By this time, a good month of his vacation had gone by.

The home we lived in at the time was laid out such that from the hallway we were papering, you could see clearly into the family room, where the TV was. It was about this time that Eric noticed that not only did I not ever ask any of his siblings to help with the wallpapering project, they were at this particular moment sitting down watching a movie.

"Mom?"

"Yes."

"Why am I the only one having to help with the wallpaper?"

This was the moment. I turned to him and said, "I wanted to prove to you that you were not lazy." I explained that he had worked hard, with a good attitude, on a job that is difficult and frustrating, and he did it for a month without realizing he was the only one being asked. To this day, the word "lazy" does not pass his lips.

There is power in working together as a family. When families work together, great life lessons are taught, unity is built, and memories are made. First of all, your children see you working just as hard and with the same standards you require from them. It cements what you are teaching them and gives validity to the standards by which you judge their work. And just like the individual chores, family projects have real life applications. I believe that working together is a cornerstone for teaching children the value of being a "team player," while also giving them lessons on how to be a leader. They learn how to evaluate skills against what needs to be done, how to delegate, and what it means to work together. Instead of leaving the job when their assigned tasks are done, they learn to look around and see what is needed or who needs their help until the work is complete.

When Stephanie got married, we decided we wanted twinkle lights on the trees at the outdoor reception venue, so we asked to meet up with a more knowledgeable person to discuss stringing the lights. All I had to do was bring some help, so I brought my children. They ranged in age from 8 to 21. Due to a miscommunication, we soon realized we would be doing the actual light-draping ourselves. I turned to the kids and said, "Help." They were on it. Because they were used to working together, delegating, and accepting assignments, they quickly got organized and had a couple dozen trees wrapped with lights in under an hour. Working together in this way created a bond and made the reception all the more fun as we talked about how lovely the trees looked and laughed as we retold the story.

As mothers, we figure out our system to clean and organize our house. We tell the children what their responsibilities are within that system and then hold them accountable. But as the children get older, letting them have a say in this process teaches great problem-solving skills and outside-the-box reasoning. I like to call it the "or" solution. When Rich and I are discussing possible solutions to a problem, I love when one of us says the word "or." What follows is usually a more creative or effective way of solving the problem. By having our children identify why doing a job or task is so difficult, and having them come up with the "or" (i.e., another way to accomplish the same thing), we gain opportunities to teach this needful skill.

I can remember an "or" moment with my sons, Eric and Daniel, who were ages 13 and 11 at the time. I love to do laundry. I know, I know; it is the never-ending story because there is always more to do. But, I enjoy the doing. We have lived many places, but when we lived in Indiana, I had the best set-up. The laundry room was part of the large finished basement I mentioned earlier. In addition, there was a play area, a place for me to spread out my sewing projects, and a bedroom for Eric and Daniel. Every Monday was laundry day and I only had that one goal to accomplish. I would spend the day in the basement with my children as I went through the various stages of cleaning the clothes. The busyness of life slowed down to a peaceful pace and all was right with the world.

I had a system. The kids would bring the dirty clothes down to the basement in their laundry baskets. After their clothes were washed, I would fold and put the clean clothes back into the baskets and they would take them back to their rooms and put the clothes away. This last step is where the wheels of this well-run machine fell off; the birds stopped chirping and like a needle being scraped along a record, the happy music would stop.

As I mentioned, Eric and Daniel had the bedroom in the basement. It was a mystery to me how the two kids who had to take their laundry across the room could never get any of the clothes out of the baskets and into their dresser drawers. The next week they would hand me their laundry baskets, dirty clothes mixed in with the clean clothes from the previous week. Grrrrr. I would ask them why they could not just put them away? Week after week after week. They gave me their reasons (none of which made any sense to me), but when I finally listened to them, motivated by my desire to actually solve the problem versus simply making them do it "right," they came up with the "or."

I bought three additional baskets. One was for underwear, one for shirts, and one for pants. When the basket of clean clothes made it to their room, they took the items out and dispersed them into their "clean clothes" baskets, which became their de facto dresser drawers. It isn't how I wanted to do it, but it worked. Because it was a problem they identified and helped solve, they were committed to making the plan a success.

Last of all, I want to consider the power of working one-on-one alongside our children. This allows for some wonderful teaching moments and opportunities to make memories, but in addition, it provides added depth to your relationship as you learn to know each other in a different way.

With my fifth child, I realized that our family had outgrown the small round table in our dining room. We were a few years out of graduate school with little money. I asked the Lord if He would help me find a table we could afford, one that was big enough for all of us to sit around with enough space leftover to fit the food. A few weeks later, I found a seven-foot by almost-three-foot table sitting in the attic of an antique store at an unbelievably good price.

It needed some varnish, so I quickly rubbed on a few quick coats and put the table into action. I found that I needed to repeat this process about once a year to keep up with the constant wiping and scrubbing. After three or four years of this, I realized I needed to start from scratch. Stephanie helped me move the table out of the kitchen and we began the laborious task of sanding down all of the previous layers of stain and varnish until we had it down to the wood. Sanding, by itself, was a huge job and the design of the table legs required us to sand them by hand, rather than using an electric sander. After the sanding came the varnish. Trying to apply varnish down a seven-foot table, without streaks, brush marks or bubbles was no small task. Each layer had to be completely dry before the next coat was added. It took about a week before the table looked like new.

There were positive things that came out of that project. I had a beautiful table that would hold up to daily use, and Stephanie learned new skills she uses today. But the best thing that happened was a friendship that was created while we talked and laughed and worked side-by-side. As my family at home has grown smaller and Stephanie's has grown larger, this table, full of memories, is now in her dining room, blessing her and her family.

I asked the question at the beginning of the chapter: "Why do our children have to do chores?" As mothers, we constantly have to evaluate what we fight for and what we let go. I will say that although you may not know it while in the throes of all that you are doing, there is power in chores. One mom to another, hang in there. The truth is, children complain. It doesn't matter what they are being asked to do. If you had them do nothing, they would complain about having nothing to do.

We have to look over and beyond all of that to what we are trying to accomplish and against all odds, stick to our beliefs. We think our children are never going to "get it." But one day, the child who complained about having to clean the bathroom will call you up from college and complain about the roommate who thinks all toilets clean themselves. The child who never liked cleaning his or her room will call you up and complain about their roommate who throws everything on the floor. Or, as happened to me one day while Daniel was serving his mission, I got a call from the mission secretary who had partnered with Daniel and his companion to get an apartment ready for a new missionary. She said that Daniel looked things over and said, "This place needs the Cindy Anderson treatment." He then set about cleaning the place top to bottom, including grabbing a knife, covering it with a wash rag and cleaning the entire fridge, including all the cracks and crevices. She told me it was clear to her that Daniel had been taught how to work.

At the end of this chapter, you may have the impression that my home was always clean. It wasn't. I have seven children; toys were out for them to play with, backpacks, homework and other projects in varying stages were on various tables. Sports equipment and clothes, winter boots and other items as they went in and out during the day were sometimes littered in front of the door. Often after a long day, I washed my dinner dishes in the morning. But, we all had jobs, chores, tasks, and projects we worked on together to keep our home as clean and organized as possible, given the "real life" part of life. And although a clean home is wonderful, it wasn't the point. There are a lot of ways to keep your house clean and in order. But to teach your children how to rule the world? In my opinion, there is no better way.

CHAPTER NINE

Teenagers

"The pay sounds good, but do ninjas get benefits?"

Chapter Note: *In this chapter, I can only discuss your garden variety, following-the-script teenager. I know that many parents have additional burdens that stem from a variety of circumstances, whether it be children born with disabilities, teenagers making self-destructive choices, or other similar life-altering situations. My heart goes out to you. May God walk alongside you on your challenging path. Please do not mistake anything I say here as advice or minimizing the seriousness or difficulty of your individual situations.*

*W*hen my children started turning fourteen, I noticed a very strange thing. They looked and sounded like my children, but something was off. Everything was now an argument; teenage logic was being thrown into every conversation. For example: a lie isn't a lie if you (mom) didn't ask the right question. There are others; it is head-spinning reasoning and caused us to constantly question our sanity.

It's not easy for our teenagers either. What a confusing time of life. Everything is changing; they are being assaulted with hormones and a self-awareness that causes them to second guess everything they say and do. Anxiety is covered with mock self-assuredness and they are as confused and bewildered about the changes as we are.

In some sort of paradox where logic does not exist, at the same time, they believe they have life all figured out. The conclusion is drawn that parents are no longer needed. They fire us and then can't figure out why we keep showing up for work. They don't understand why their parents don't just let them make their own choices and live their own lives. They would be surprised to hear that we do want them to grow up, become independent, and be able to navigate their way through the world; we just disagree on the way to get there.

When one of my children turned 14, I turned to Rich and said, "Hold on, this is going to be a wild ride." And it was. What do we do to help our children get through these tumultuous years and out the other side? I have outlined a few suggestions.

1. Don't be afraid to say NO.

I want to make it clear that in this case, I am talking about the definition of no that comes from the Old English meaning "not ever." On a scale between no and yes, there are many things our children ask to do or go to in which a discussion is needed before a decision is made. This kind of give-and-take is healthy and often what starts out to be a no ends up being a yes, or a yes with some conditions. That is not what I am talking about here.

The word "not ever" is used to defend truth and your predetermined moral code. We use it when we know there is danger. Not allowing them to play in the street is a good example. We use it when saying yes would be detrimental to them and those around them. No they cannot hit, lock the dog in a closet, yell at the top of their lungs, get up on the tables at a restaurant and begin a full-fledged run, jumping from table to table around the restaurant while I (I mean, some mother) chase the child and tell him to get down. (That might be a true story.)

Teaching our children to understand and accept "no" is fundamental to our ability to teach them what they need to know. If they think that "no" is merely a suggestion, nothing you say or try to have them do will be taken seriously. Learning to accept and react appropriately to a "no, not ever" is a skill they need for adulthood. Jumping up and down or whining to their boss until she changes her mind isn't going to fly. They will move into their adult world, unable to take a "no" from anyone.

It's not the saying no that is so hard, it's the sticking to it that is. When working with our teenagers, there are times when the courage it would take to step in front of a moving train to save our child is less than the courage it takes to stand by a "no, not ever."

Why do I say this? Because every no has a price. The arguments, the why nots, the attempts to negotiate, the histrionics and drama make it easier to just say yes in the short term, but again, motherhood is a long game.

One of my daughters wanted to go to a party with her friends. I listened to what she had to say and after a very few short questions, I responded with the dreaded "no." She was prepared for this and

100

began following me around the house telling me none of my reasons made sense and began "solving" all of my problems with the party proposition. For example, I told her she couldn't go because there was not going to be parental supervision.

"Her brother will be there and he is 18." Problem solved. (No. Not at all.)

At a certain point, I decided it was enough and had to declare that the conversation was over. Clearly not understanding my statement, she tried one last, in her mind, inarguable argument.

"But all of my friends' mothers are letting them go!" I took a deep breath.

"Well, then I guess if you don't learn anything else from this, you will learn that I do not bend to peer pressure."

She was upset; in teenage drama language, she was "distraught." She swore to never speak to me again, which if I am being honest, I wasn't all that upset about at the time. As it usually does, her mindset changed the next day when she needed something. Mad isn't permanent.

2. Choose your battles.

I am a firm believer in the "choose your battles" theory when it comes to kids. You simply can't fight about everything. Well, you could, but it wouldn't be enjoyable. Deciding when to raise the flag for battle and when to let things go is as easy as an elephant trying to walk the tightrope. What matters and what doesn't? What is worth the fight and what isn't?

An example of something I didn't raise a flag for was hair. I didn't care: long, short, curly, red, purple or green. My philosophy was: "Do what you gotta do." And they did. Sooner or later (mostly later), they figured out what looked good and what didn't. I just wasn't going to fight about it.

One of our flags of battle was dating. Our children didn't date until they were 16. That was a hard and fast rule. We didn't budge.

My teenaged Stephanie was asked out on a date and she wanted to go. I should say here that she was closer to 16 than 15. However, when she asked if she could go, the answer was no. She asked if we could discuss it again and began laying out her perspective.

"I am a good kid." True, but not the point.

"You can trust me." Also true.

"What do you think I am going to do a few months before I am sixteen that I wouldn't do afterwards?" Not relevant.

On and on the discussion went. She was not being argumentative, just persistent. A few days into this discussion, I picked her up from high school and was beginning to drive out of the parking lot.

"Please, mom. Why can't I just go?"

I was tired, I was weakening. Some of what she said made some sense. I took a breath to say "yes" and I heard, not out loud, but in my head, *her* voice scream "NO. Don't say yes. Don't give in." For a brief moment, my perspective was lengthened, and I could picture the positive outcomes in my daughter's life that would result from her seeing me stand by my convictions. What was to be a yes stayed a no. The warning to stand firm on an issue we chose to battle over taught me to believe that our children rely on us to be consistent and firm. It encouraged me to back up my previous answer and not be afraid to say no. You don't know it because they are very convincing as they scream and cry and pout and try to bargain, but the truth is, they are counting on us to do the right thing even when they think it's not what they want. As our children get older and become parents themselves, they can see those battles from a new perspective and are grateful for the example of "standing your ground" you gave them.

3. Remind them you are all on the same team.

William and his wife, Jamie, have a family motto of sorts. Sometimes they remind each other, "We are all on the same team." One day, Will and Jamie were "discussing" the best plan for a family activity and four-year-old Ellie didn't like that they could not agree. She went over to them and said, "Same team, guys, same team."

When our children are facing uncertainty or problems they cannot solve on their own, it is important that they know we are their allies (same team) and not their adversaries.

Out of frustration, I once told sixteen-year-old Melanie that she didn't appreciate my wisdom. "If you would just do what I tell you, everything in your life would work out." She was sixteen; it fell on deaf ears. As much as we would love to sit our children down and give them the benefit of all of our years lived, impart our wisdom and give them a how-to list to follow, it doesn't work that way.

Being an ally means we often do more listening than talking, giving our children an opportunity and a safe place to voice what is happening in their lives from their perspective.

Being an ally doesn't mean we don't ever have to use consequences nor do we have to protect them from our disappointment in their choices. Conversely, we don't let our disappointment be the only thing they feel. If we follow up quickly with love and concern and a sincere desire to help them, we reinforce that we are all on the same team. They can trust that we have their backs regardless of what they do. Even if we are disappointed, we will support them and help them face life situations successfully, including the consequences. Working through this cycle of conflict and resolve helps our children to fear confrontations less and teaches them how to come back from disappointment, arguments, or a difference of opinion.

When Michael was 14, he started seminary. His teacher was young and inexperienced in dealing with teenagers in general, and a group of teenage boys specifically. As 14-year-old boys do, they smell weakness and the teacher's inexperienced reactions to their behavior only solidified for these boys their justification for acting up.

The problem soon escalated and parents were consulted. We approached Michael and asked him about seminary and his teacher.

The list of his teacher's failings was pretty long as he tried to justify his behavior. We took this opportunity to help Michael see things from his teacher's point of view. The behavior of Michael and his friends showed a disrespect that wasn't acceptable and needed to change.

We coached him and supported him in trying different ways of communicating. We encouraged him to find ways to get to know his teacher as a person. Over the course of time, things got better and three years later, this same man was asked to work with Michael's youth group at church. This time, it was very different. Michael was now a little older and wiser, but the efforts he made to resolve the earlier situation had enabled a friendship to form with this leader. Michael now had a respect and an appreciation for him and humility for what he had learned through the process. Michael accepted the consequences of his actions, knew that we were disappointed in his choices, but also knew that we were a team, working together to solve and resolve the problem.

4. Widen their view.

Teenagers have tunnel vision. At the end of the tunnel, there is a sign that says "me." When Rich and I were confronted with this truth, the question we asked ourselves was, "how do we help them turn their signs over so that instead of 'me,' it says 'them?'" We decided giving our children opportunities to serve others would be a good way to accomplish that goal.

If Rich or I were serving, we would sign the kids up to come along as well. If someone needed help and if it was something our children could do (babysit, help clean, yard work, organized service projects, etc.), we would volunteer them for service. Someone asked me how I was so sure my kids would do what I had just volunteered them for. I laughed and told them they were used to it. Did my children thank me in song for the opportunity to serve others? No. Often they were grumpy as I asked them to "turn over their sign," but they went, and more times than not, my children who left grumpy came home happy and grateful they were able to help.

Serving others allows them to experience the unique feeling of love that enters our heart for the person or people we are serving and for the people we are serving with. When they experience rubbing shoulders with others and being part of something larger than themselves, it expands their world and perspective. The things they think they are entitled to become blessings. When you deliver food to people in dire circumstances, they (our kids) complain less about what they're having for dinner. The troubles they may be having at the time become smaller and easier with the understanding that others suffer more. They learn to look outward as you encourage them to help someone load their groceries in their car or pick up and return things people dropped. They watch you treat others with kindness regardless of their circumstance and begin to emulate that in their own lives. As we served together as a family, the shared experience pulled us closer together; we helped our children learn to reach outward, look for ways to help, and be willing to take time out of their day to help someone else have a better day. With every act of service, children gain an intuitive ability to find ways to help others. Thinking of others becomes a permanent and natural part of their lives.

When William was 16, he, Rich, two other leaders and his varsity boy scout troop all went on a canoeing trip to the Boundary Waters National Canoe Area on the Minnesota/Ontario border. Boundary Waters is a series of long, almost connected lakes requiring both water and land travel. The plan was to canoe and portage 15 or 20 miles through a series of beautiful, clear lakes over three or four days. For those of you who do not go canoeing, a portage is when you come up on land and carry the boat and its cargo between two navigable waters. On this trip, they were split up into teams of two people per canoe. When a team came to a portage, they would carry the heavy aluminum canoe from one body of water to another, all while wearing their packs. Rich and William were on a team together.

Rich has a muscle metabolic syndrome that left unheeded has, in the past, caused temporary kidney failure. The muscular strain of carrying the canoe from point A to point B, combined with dehydration of the muscles, caused a flare up of this syndrome. It became evident to William that Rich was having a hard time. Without being asked, he began to serve his father. William would take their canoe to the next entrance point while Rich waited back with the packs. Then, Will would go back for his dad and they would walk together with their packs up the trail to the canoe. This unspoken service and act of love from William made it possible for Rich to give his muscles the needed rest to avoid complications. William did this graciously, a display of his growth, without complaint or teasing.

5. Build your time bombs.

When Caroline was a baby, Rich took the older children on a day hike. We lived in Ohio and one of our favorite hiking places was the William McKinley Memorial Park. There is a trail along a creek that is about 4-5 feet wide and at some point in the hike, it became necessary to cross it. Rich found a place that had some good stepping stones and, one by one, Rich would grab each child's hand as soon as he could and help them balance as they made their way to the other side. Melanie, who is usually fearless, was a little nervous about stepping on the stones and chose to continue walking on the opposite side for a while. Finally, without warning, Rich heard Melanie yell, "I'm coming!" With a running start, she jumped what seemed to be straight up in the air and came crashing down in the middle of the creek. Rich was not prepared to have her jump like that and as a result, she came down with a crash, got banged up, and Rich got wet trying to help her out of the stream.

To me, this describes the sudden jolt into the teenage years. When they are young, we show them the safe places to cross and help them keep their balance. When they turn into teenagers, they yell, "I'm coming," sometimes make an ill-fated leap, and we are not prepared.

106

We teach, we preach, we follow them around, we remind them over and over what we have been trying to say, and we give them good advice, to no avail. When they don't respond to being told over and over again, we devise ways to make them learn. We charge them money for leaving wet towels on the floor, ground them if their room isn't clean, remind them that mothers have feelings, too. No matter how hard we try to show them, they won't cross over an easy path of rocks.

We worry that our children may never learn what they need to know. But they do. For instance, we would have family nights where all of the teenagers sat, pouted, and looked bored and then (to our surprise) wanted to talk about the gospel while we ate dessert.

"I know . . . that for many of your students [children], you are in fact planting little intellectual and spiritual time bombs, and the implantation is so subtle that you'll wonder if in fact you have connected at all. And then someday, when circumstances are right, there will be in them an explosion or reminding relevancy from that implantation from your instruction."[23]

We had a steadfast rule in our home. We had to meet the friend and their parents before our children could go to anyone's home (or out with anyone). The friend we had to meet in person, the parents, if not in person, then at least through a phone call. My children hated (strong word, but appropriate) that rule.

"Mom, you were right," my son, William, told me recently.

I knew I was (Aren't moms always right?), but was curious as to which time he was referring to.

"What was I right about?"

Ellie, his daughter who was about nine, loves making friends. She was telling her dad that she wanted to go to this friend's house

---

23 Neal A. Maxwell, "The Old Testament: Relevancy within Antiquity" (presentation; CES Symposium on the Old Testament; Provo, UT; August 16, 1979). © By Intellectual Reserve, Inc.

and that friend's party. He heard himself say the word "no." And when Ellie asked why, he said, "Ellie, we need to meet your friends and their parents first." (Music to my ears.)

He said, "I never understood that rule until now." The thought of sending her off without knowing whom she was with or who would be in charge set off a panic in him and he realized, once more, that mom was right. (Yes, I needed to emphasize that point again.)

This is one example of a time bomb going off, however they can detonate in a variety of ways:

1. It can be a change of perspective, like we saw when William became a father.

2. It can happen when they get out on their own and start realizing they really don't know everything. They adopt philosophies and habits that let you see they were actually listening.

3. Sometimes, they present one of your ideas (which you were sure they would never get) as their own philosophy, as if they had never heard it before, and wonder why you didn't tell them. (Sigh.)

4. You may hear a compliment from a teacher or parent when they express how polite and helpful your child is and you wonder whose child they are talking about.

Somewhere deep inside, the things we teach them are being recorded, set with timers to explode at just the right moment. This is the most important long game you will ever play. If you come to conclusions about their future life based solely on their choices as a teenager, you take out any hope of progressing, learning, or maturing on your child's part. Melanie got banged up and bruised after her impromptu leap, but she recovered. The bruises and scrapes healed and what was traumatic at the time is now looked back on fondly and with humor.

Understanding the genius of these time bombs, we can purposely build them, knowing what we do now will affect them later. We can seek out teaching moments, then trust, despite their reaction or behavior, that the time bombs have been set and will go off at the right time.

6. Say yes more and no less.

Yes, I know what I just said, but I am not talking about the "not ever-no." In our efforts to prepare our children for the "real world," sometimes the need we have to make sure they understand the realities of life causes us to miss out on some real relationship-building moments.

Michael, age four at the time, came to me one day with the weight of the world on his shoulders. After asking him what was on his mind he said, "I don't know what to be when I grow up: a fighter-fighter (firefighter), an artist, or a ninja." It was easy to assure him that he had time to choose. With our teenagers, we tend to start stamping out the "impossible." If Michael had given me those same choices as a teenager, I might have pointed out the lack of jobs for ninjas and how hard it would be to support a family being an artist. As parents, we contribute to their self-esteem when we acknowledge, rejoice, include ourselves in, and in a realistic way, support their passions. We can encourage them to try things out, develop their talents, and see what they can do. I have heard the common phrase, "Decide what you love to do and then figure out a way to make a living doing it." This is a much better reaction than telling your son about the lack of ninja jobs. It took me a couple kids to learn this concept. Eric, age 14, came to me one day:

"Mom, I know what I want to be when I grow up."

"What?"

"A trash man."

"Really, why?"

"I only have to work once a week and get paid a lot of money."

I pointed out that on the days they were not collecting our trash, they were in other neighborhoods working very hard for their well-earned living. Dream crushed.

When you say no less often, your children open up and start telling you things they might never have otherwise. Some of my favorite conversations with my children happened in their teenage years. They see the world so differently than we do; their humor is at the least interesting and at best, really funny. Their imaginations are always going and because they believe they are immortal and have the world all figured out, they have nothing but possibilities ahead of them. We get to witness the development of who they are and who they are going to be. Love them up, have fun.

Our teenagers test the boundaries while counting on us to hold them to the line. They are pushing us away while praying we don't go. They act like they don't want a hug from you and yet stand so close to you, you think you will fall down. They act like they don't care about school, but want you to know when they do something of notice. They make fun of their siblings while defending them to others. They say they don't need you, only later to tell people how much you mean to them.

An adult will come out of this. Stay alert, stay off the crooked path of teenage logic as best you can, and just like we did when they were babies, watch them sleep and remember all the reasons you love them.

CHAPTER TEN

Top Five Lessons to Live By

"Children can still hear you even when they aren't listening. (It's their superpower.)"

*F*rom the lighthearted to the serious, I am frequently asked a variety of questions about motherhood. No matter the question, each mom is really asking, "How did you teach your children to navigate adult life?" I believe that there is no one right answer to that. We all have the same purpose and end goal in mind, but there are a lot of roads to get there. As I list the top five teaching priorities of the Anderson Family, think of you, your family and goals, and begin a top five list for yourself.

1. Life isn't fair.

"That's not fair," my children cry. They are mad, mad at me. They think I am being unkind, and treating them with less love and consideration than their siblings. There is unfairness in life, but I would say that a number of the perceived injustices in their childhood are less about being "fair" and more about "taking turns." This is an important distinction. It is critical to recognize unfairness in the world and to stand up for injustice or for someone who cannot stand up for themselves. But if our children learn to "take their turn," it teaches them a myriad of skills that can arm them for success. They develop the ability to perceive and evaluate situations. This perspective allows them to choose what actions they should or should not take, given the circumstances.

As an example: birthdays are often seen as unfair. The children whose birthday it is not get green-eyed by the presents and attention their sibling is receiving. Remind them birthdays are special days. Talk about how much they enjoy their birthday and how it would feel to have to share it with their siblings. Understanding the concept of taking turns allows our children to learn how to celebrate and encourage others, and teaches them the ability to be happy for someone else.

Sometimes, my children would come home from school to find out that their younger sibling was given a new toy or some kind of treat during the day. They would run to me, asking:

"What did you get for me?"

"Nothing."

"That's not fair!"

"If you loved me, you would buy me a toy, too," or, "You love (name of sibling) more than me." With this kind of perceived personal affront, how could they come to any other conclusion? However, if we teach them to look at a problem through a different view, perhaps they could think about their sibling who would have rather been at home playing instead of being dragged around from store to store, often to buy things for the child that is upset. From that perspective, it might seem completely fair for mom to do something special for that particular child. They had their turn being the little one at home and often received a fun lunch, treat or toy while out during an errand day.

A child's life is often perceived as unfair when they see a sibling being treated differently than they were, in similar situations. I mothered my children all the same, according to my personality and our family's goals and ideals, but no two children are the same and I tried to make allowances for the individuality and personality of each child.

There are reasons for inconsistency. Children who are more responsible have more privileges. Interests and abilities are different. I had some children who intuitively knew how to study and some who didn't. Those who figured it out on their own didn't require any help from me. Those that didn't had to have more supervision.

Learning not to cry out in protest every time something is done differently or changes from child to child teaches our children to understand when and under what circumstances exceptions should or could be made. When our mothering adapts to their individual needs, they learn that their individuality is valued and considered. This helps them to judge circumstances and people as individuals, instead of throwing out blanket judgments before knowing all of the facts.

And, we teach our children that there are times life is unfair. When William was in the fourth grade, his class was assigned to build a structure out of everyday materials. There were rules, along with size requirements, and a list of what materials could be used. In capital letters and bold print, the instructions said that the students were to do this on their own, no parental help. It was to be judged and prizes given out, with points taken off if a hint of parental help was given. William did a great job, getting zero hands-on help from mom and dad. The day it was due came and because of the size of his project, it was necessary for me to take him to school and help him carry it in. As we turned the corner and walked down the corridor to his classroom, there was a line of proud parents as they carried their complicated, couldn't-have-been-touched-by-a-child projects into the classroom. The teacher praised each child as they brought in their parents' work. William's looked like he had spent two hours instead of two weeks building his. What should I have done? Should I have made a fuss? Should I have taken him and his project home in protest? It wasn't "fair" that the parents had used the letter the teacher had sent home to line their wastebaskets. Nor was it fair that William's work was to be judged against the parents'. It wasn't fair that the teacher, after saying what the rules were, did not take off points or disqualify any of the projects. I looked at William's face and he looked at mine. I smiled and helped him place his offering down and told him I was proud of him for following the rules.

Life isn't always fair and not everyone follows the rules. It's a fact of life. But, if we allow our children to dwell on it or be angry about it, they don't learn to put it in its proper perspective. In this case, William had to move past the unfairness of the situation and learn to find as much satisfaction in doing what's right, which William did, as in winning first place, which William did not.

2. You can't teach your children how to succeed if you don't first teach them how to fail.

There are a lot of ways we can accomplish this. I have chosen to concentrate on two of them. The first one is: teach your children that "failure" is another word for trying.

First and foremost, when something we plan and try doesn't work, the idea has failed, not the person. Taking focus off of themselves helps them see failure for what it is. We can teach them how to learn from what didn't work, make a plan and try again. This process helps our children learn they can rise above failure, succeed, and come out better than they started.

When our children are faced with problems, we have an opportunity to show them we are there for them. We can coach them, discuss ideas and solutions, but success comes from them and their ability to carry out plans and work through their problems: a skill they will need to help make their way through life.

When our children are little, they face a challenge and we fix it. We move things out of their way when they begin to walk so they don't fall down. When an older sibling takes their toy, we make them give it back. We do these things without thinking. At age-appropriate times, we can help them make the transition from us solving their problems to teaching them the skills needed for them to solve their own. This includes, at times, standing by and watching them fail (I am not talking about bullying or life- or soul-threatening situations.), then helping them pick themselves up, evaluate what happened, and make a plan to do something different the next try.

I read an article by Margarita Tartakovsky, M.S. called "10 Tips for Raising Resilient Kids." She talks about how mothers sometimes try to make sure that their children are always comfortable. She points out that in those efforts, we often try to stay a step ahead and an-

116

ticipate everything our children are going to run into. The problem with that is that life, with its unpredictability and hair pin twists and turns, makes that very thing impossible. She explains, "A parent's responsibility to their children isn't to be there all of the time, it is to teach them to handle uncertainty and to problem solve."[24]

When we moved to Texas, Daniel was 12 years old. It was his first year in middle school and instead of being with the children he had grown up with, he found himself in the position of being the new kid, without friends. Classes were not the challenge, but every day, he had to face the lunch period with the same inner struggle. Faced with the reality that he would need to find a place to sit, Daniel scanned the faces and asked himself, "Who do I dare ask to sit by or do I risk sitting by myself and being called a loser?" His solution to avoid this was to find the longest lunch line, hoping that by the time he got through it, there would be only minutes left to eat.

Daniel had grown up with the kids he knew from kindergarten; the skill of making friends had not been developed. Every day after our move, we would talk about what happened and discuss new things to try, and every day, he came home defeated. Lunch period was a daily failure and Daniel wanted to quit. His easy solution was to suggest that he move back to Indiana where all his friends were.

Every day, I sent him to school knowing he would have to face "lunch period." I wanted to pick him up from school early, call and change his schedule, or tell him he could stay home. But I didn't. I knew that the only one who could solve this was Daniel.

There was no easy fix to this problem. It took months before things began to turn around. Coming home on the bus, Daniel finally got up the courage to make a friend. Alex Anderson lived in our neighborhood and an instant friendship was formed. Alex

---

24 Margarita Tartakovsky, M.S., "10 Tips for Raising Resilient Kids," Psych Central. July 17, 2016. https://psychcentral.com/lib/10-tips-for-raising-resilient-kids/

introduced him to his friends, Ben and Kyle. (All three of the boys are still friends to this day.) With the success he had with Alex, he gained confidence in his ability to make friends. He felt like if Alex, Ben, and Kyle liked him, perhaps others would, too.

What started out to be a weakness became a strength as Daniel continued to put himself outside of his comfort zone and make friends. Lunch time was no longer a challenge; he found plenty of people to sit with and looks back on that time in his life fondly.

By solving this problem on his own, he had the confidence to reach out past his friends from his cross country team or academic interests. Daniel, remembering what it felt like to be left out or nervous in a social setting, would make friends in all of the "social groups" in school. He looked for the person who didn't seem to fit and reached out in friendship, becoming known in school as a friend to everyone.

In his senior year of high school, he broke the mold of the typical winner and was elected Homecoming King. At the end of that year, he won Mr. KHS. Both of those events stemmed from him taking a risk on his own and developing the skills to be friends not to just to one, but to many. This experience has continued to be an influence in Daniel's life. What started out to be a problem too big to solve has led to a social life complete with interesting and amazing friendships.

The second way we help our children learn to succeed by failing is: teach them that winning or losing, we must be graceful at both.

We can teach our children that doing our best does not guarantee a win. Past that, we teach them how to come back from a loss gracefully and learn to use the loss to learn what to do better next time.

Wanting to win, to be first, is an instinct we come with into this world. I can't tell you how many times I would hear the children outside yelling at each other after some sort of competition.

"I won and you didn't."

"No you didn't, you tripped me!"

"Ha, ha! I won. You are too slow!"

"I am not too slow!"

The shoving would start and they would all, in unison, yell, "MOM!!!"

For the most part, people like to win. Competitions of all types are set up to have a winning team or person. My children are runners. They have run marathons, track, and cross country. Like all athletes, they take their sport seriously and are out to win.

William was the first in a long line of my children who ran cross country. For those of you not familiar with the sport, it is both an individual and a team sport. Runners are judged on individual times and teams by a points-scoring method.

After a high school cross country meet in which my son William placed second, I said to him, "Great job." It was too soon. He looked at me and said, "Second place really just means you are the first loser." I looked around at my other kids for some support and they all kind of nodded their heads and said William was right. I get that. You go into something and do your best and you fall short of the goal and it doesn't feel good. But it isn't an excuse to behave badly.

Even though William was upset at himself, he congratulated the winner, took compliments, and gave compliments to his team. It is ok to be disappointed, but it is not ok to be self-centered. Nor is it ok when the types of arguments I described in the backyard with siblings get transferred to any arena of competition. "The coach didn't play me enough." "We were better, the ref was making bad calls." "The course was messed up," and on and on they go. The excuses for the loss lay at the feet of others while the bad loser has no shared responsibility or camaraderie with his team. But, if children can accept the win or loss as a team, and not a personal insult to them and their abilities, they would learn important losing skills for success. They would be actively engaged in conversations with their team, learn to commiserate, and become familiar with the process of deciding as a team what to do better next time. Success or a win would feel sweeter;

119

TOP FIVE LESSONS TO LIVE BY

their plan was executed and successful. When loss is looked at as "everyone's fault but my own," everything is a competition: failing a test, being wrong in an argument or not getting your way. Nothing is lost gracefully. To lose gracefully and make each loss a productive lesson in what can be done better is one of the most important things our children learn.

3. We can choose our choices, but we cannot choose our consequences.

"What will happen if I throw this?" "What will you do if I don't go to bed?" Children like to know ahead of time what the results of their wrong choices might be. To that question, I would answer, "You can choose your choices, but you can't choose your consequences."

I like the relationship of choice and consequence. You make a right choice, which results in a good consequence, or you can make a wrong choice, resulting in an undesired consequence. A person shows that they have learned when their behavior changes. A consistent cause-and-effect vs. arbitrary or reactionary punishment helps them to learn and apply the principles you are teaching. In addition, it helps our children navigate their world, make better choices, and take responsibility for the choices they make.

Once, Stephanie came in late from being out with friends. She had not called to let me know where she was or why she was going to be late. I started questioning her with the usual "where were you?" and "why were you late?" questions. She looked at me and said, "I decided to stay late and didn't think you would let me. I know there is a consequence and that I am grounded for two weeks." I agreed and she went up to bed. I smiled an evil mother smile, knowing I would have only grounded her for one week.

The story I just told is an exception to a rule. It can be exhausting trying to get to a place where your child admits their wrong choice. They take you around the barn with half-truths, whole lies, and as many shaded interpretations of the facts as they can possibly come up with. By the time you are done, there is a consequence for lying and a consequence probably a bit larger than you would have given for what they did wrong. If only you hadn't had to give hours of your time you will never get back chasing the truth.

But, they can eventually learn that not only does the world not end once a consequence is given and accepted, once the consequence is over there is satisfaction in making something right. This process helps them learn not to fear the consequence more than a desire to make things right.

4. Some boredom in life isn't a bad thing.

One day, Melanie said to me, "Mom, I'm bored. What can I do? And don't give me any chores!" We give our children opportunities for growth and achievement when we teach them the skill and the benefits of being bored.

We are less adept at knowing what to do with downtime or empty space since the influence of technology now makes us feel we are entitled to fast action and instant search results. The changes in our world cause a divide regarding the differences between childhoods like mine: summers spent sans cell phones/videos; riding through the neighborhood on my bike after breakfast with friends inventing games; adventures; and wonderful creations, compared to a world that is becoming increasingly unsafe for this type of unsupervised, imaginative play. These factors, among others, contribute to our decreased ability to know where and how to use unspent energy.

Boredom in and of itself, without the contributing factors I mentioned, can be looked at as an undesirable thing. After all, it's when our children are bored and can't figure out what to do that they usually get into trouble, start fighting, and someone gets hurt. Mom steps in, solves the boredom problem and the children learn that it is Mom's job to provide them with their happiness and entertainment.

There are times when a child says they are bored that we can give them a little attention, snuggle time, or offer to do something together, but we keep from our children the benefits and positive results of dealing with boredom if we always step in. Boredom helps children develop creativity, contributes to self-discovery of interests, satisfies curiosity, and encourages their ability to quiet down the world, take a breath and think about absolutely nothing.

I can't tell you as a child how many carnivals I planned, or about the time I decided to try and dig a hole in my backyard deep enough to see China. My friends and I would make up "and then you said" plays. You know, the kind where you put together a story and orally write the script as you go. I would draw, paint, read, or just lie under a tree and think about life and my place in it.

What things do your children enjoy doing? What are their gifts and talents? I am not an advocate of no screens, but as we limit the screen time, entertainment, and other activities that mainly involve observation, children can have time during the day that they can spend playing, working on interests, gifts and talents. Over time, they will develop things to do when they find themselves with "nothing to do." And if not, there is always a list of chores.

5. Don't let them use other people's bad behavior as an excuse for their own.

One day, one of my teenagers was being a bit sassy. I replied with my classic line, "Do you want to try and say that again?" If those words came out of my mouth, they knew they had one chance to think carefully, adjust, and try again before consequences began. Her response was that I should feel lucky, even though she was being a bit sassy, because "her other friends talked way worse to their parents." I told her, "Don't use other people's bad behavior as an excuse for your own." And so it became one of the standard things I would say.

"What you are wearing is not modest."

"My friend's dress is shorter than mine."

"Don't use other people's bad behavior as an excuse for your own."

"Don't hit your brother."

"He hit me!"

"Don't use other people's bad behavior as an excuse for your own."

Rich tells the story of a time when he was a little boy. He was making a small boat out of paper and sailing it in the gutter in front of his house while people were watering their lawns one morning. At first, with only one neighbor watering, there really wasn't enough flow in the gutter to propel the boat, which was frustrating. Happily, a few more neighbors soon joined in and his boat started rolling down the "river!" Then, disaster struck! Rich recounts, "Before I could pluck it out of the gutter, it fell into a sewer inlet, and I had heard enough about sewers to know not to try and retrieve it from there!"

It was just a summer morning's entertainment suffering a premature death, but let's think about this story in relation to the principle of our moral agency. It seems to me that as we bend to peer pressure, feeling compelled to be like everyone else, we begin to resemble that hapless little paper boat. We sometimes forget the Lord gave us the potential of a powerful motor of righteous desire, the steering wheel of agency, and the Spirit as a perfect navigation system.

Our children start out so willing to be "their own little people," but life tends to teach them the social risks of being different. We need to teach them how easy it is to be swept along, following the latest fads, fashions and ways of thinking. Additionally, children need to be aware that they can be swept along by emotions and weakness, retaliating in anger when they are treated unfairly, or over-indulging their appetites and desires.

And, like that unfortunate little boat, if we are being swept along in the current of life, not daring to be "our own person," we can face crises with the frightening realization that consequences are looming that we have no power to steer around.

We can help our children navigate all of these avenues, learn to accept responsibility for their actions, and give them the skills to see through the entire choice scenario and choose wisely, making and accepting every choice they make as their own.

As your top five list evolves, keep in mind that in the throes of raising my children, even though these things were taught and emphasized, the results of what we taught often didn't show up until later. If you get to the end of this chapter and think, "I am doing some of these things, but I don't see them working," don't be discouraged. Children can still hear you even when they aren't listening. (It's their superpower.) Have confidence, faith in yourself, and above all, stay focused on the long game.

CHAPTER ELEVEN

Be the Best Mom Your Kids Ever Had

"Math never lies."

*M*y son Michael tells me, "You are the best mom I ever had." Every time he tells me that, I smile. I've thought a lot about that sentence. Michael means it as a way to tell me he loves me. But, as I ponder the play-on-words, except for the obvious, I wonder what makes that true. The common applications of mothering might suggest that mothers could be interchangeable. It seems as though anyone could be capable of running a home and keeping up with the day-to-day schedule. This might suggest that my children could have had other options, which, at times, were very passionately requested. But, as I gave it some thought, I found the catch.

If motherhood was an algebraic equation (Put that in the category of sentences I thought I'd never say.), and we were trying to equal BME (Best Mom Ever), it would look like this:

$$io + ic + e = BME$$

We are the best mom our children ever had when we start with our individuality (io) and add it to the individuality of our children (ic) and the power of effort (e).

Let's look at each part of this equation in a little more detail:

Our Individuality (io)

"Each woman brings her own separate, unique strengths to the family . . . Being a daughter of God means that if you seek it, you can find your true identity. You will know who you are. This will make you free—not free from restraints, but free from doubts, anxieties, or peer pressure. You will not need to worry, 'Do I look all right?' 'Do I sound OK?' 'What do people think of me?' A conviction that you are a daughter of God gives you a feeling of comfort in your self-worth."[25]

Motherhood is not a one-size-fits-all proposition. In addition, we all mother under different circumstances. Some women have their children naturally. Some women adopt their children. Some women nurture children through their professions or church callings. There are other women who are working to put together a blended family. We may find ourselves faced with parenting on our own or maybe our children have physical or mental issues that test our strength. We use our individuality to navigate our circumstances as we magnify our abilities and modify our mothering according to the circumstances we are in. Our individuality stands as a testament to the words and a belief in the truth that "there is no one perfect way to be a good mother."[26] The truth of Elder Ballard's statement is profound. Not only is there more than one way to be a good mother, it is essential we all mother in our own way.

We are the creation of the greatest Creator. He knew the collection of attributes we would need to best navigate through our life, including mothering. The requirement for this formula is that our belief has to be stronger than our doubt. Embracing our "true identity" allows us to be the best mother our children ever had.

We don't have to do it all or be it all. It is not in the *how* but in the *doing* that we nurture. For all the meals I made, new recipes I tried, and worries that I didn't cook fancy enough food, my children always loved pancakes, bacon, and fruit best for dinner. I didn't need to make a five-course dinner; I just needed to make the dinner. Choose to believe in yourself. Figure out how you will nurture your children believing that you are enough, using

---

25 James E. Faust, "What It Means to Be a Daughter of God," *Ensign*, November 1999. © By Intellectual Reserve, Inc.

26 M. Russell Ballard, "Daughters of God," *Ensign*, May 2008. © By Intellectual Reserve, Inc.

the talents and abilities that are yours, and then invite them into your world.

If I had to teach my children lessons about life or God or try to demonstrate my love and deepen our relationship through my skills as a musician, it would be a challenge for all of us. Now, let me take them outside in the garden, and I can use that experience to teach them anything they need to know. When we nurture from a place true to ourselves, we are better and more comfortable knowing what to do and how to do it. Including our children in the things we love enables us to build a connection, love and trust that allows for many opportunities that we would not have to nurture our children any other way. Our children love knowing us. My children love knowing that if I have a day off, I will go to the zoo. I love gardening, writing, and art. They know that I will come to their games and other events. They know they could talk me into a Friday night movie party because I love film and fun. They know I love God, their father and them. How much deeper our relationships will be, and how much more effective our mothering can be when we invite our children to join us in the places that bring us joy.

Stephanie enjoys cooking and baking and is comfortable in the kitchen. During one of my visits years ago to her home in Virginia, she was going to prepare corn on the cob. Her girls were about seven, five, and three years old at the time. When it came time to shuck the corn, she pulled out a garbage can and had the girls stand around it, shucking the corn. It was wonderful to watch. The girls laughed and talked as their mother encouraged them in the chore. Fast forward a few years and it was time to make dinner. Stephanie gave each girl a job to do to help with dinner and with a precision that only comes over time, they worked together in the kitchen, cutting, chopping, and cooking until dinner was done. During that time, I watched as they once again laughed and talked. I heard Stephanie ask them questions about their day: nurturing and teaching while they went through the day-to-day chore of making a meal. Fast forward yet another few years: her daughter, Eden, came running into the kitchen. "I am running late and I am supposed to bring mashed potatoes to the Thanksgiving feast tonight at youth group. I don't think I have enough time." Stephanie said if they all worked together, they could get it done. Without thinking, Eden, Britta and Avery took over the kitchen. Potatoes were peeled, boiled and mashed as they worked together as they have always done. In the simple acts of preparing meals over the years, they were taught how to get along, work, enjoy time with their mother and create a bond tied to what will become treasured childhood memories that will last throughout their lifetimes. I don't know that Stephanie's girls love to cook like their mother, I am positive that there are nights that asking them to help doesn't go so smoothly, but over time, in her world, she was able to use something she was comfortable doing to teach them more than how to cook mashed potatoes.

Write down a list of things (it doesn't matter if there is one or fifteen) you love. Title the list, "My Unique, One-of-a-Kind Gifts and Talents." In your prayers, ask your Father in Heaven for opportunities to use and magnify those skills in your mothering.

Our Child's Individuality (ic)

It surprised me to realize that my children weren't like me. Sure, they all have traits that are like mine, but their unique personalities show up from day one and it is our blessing to get to know them, not just on the surface, but to know their souls and what they are capable of. When we use our own individuality to nurture our children as individuals, we help them see the same picture of themselves.

First, as we combine our individuality with theirs, we remind them every day to like themselves when they see us liking them, taking genuine interest in the things they love. Second, we are able to help our children learn what they are capable of when we encourage them to go beyond their self-imposed limits and rise above defeat to accomplish something. And third, when we take our children's individuality into account, our children learn that they are valued and considered in ways that are meaningful to them and their circumstances.

Caroline struggles with anxieties. These anxieties cause her to worry about issues that others would think were inconsequential. The conclusions or perceived outcomes of the anxiety are based on her worst fears. Growing up, one of her anxieties involved school. Caroline was a good student, but when it came time to take a test, her fear was that if she failed (anything below an A), it would be a complete, life-ending failure. On top of that, she worried that if she failed, our disappointment would be so profound that we would most likely stop loving her.

The state tests that the schools are required to give were the worst for Caroline. All through the year, the teachers presented the test as a do-or-die proposition. The teacher never failed to inform the kids that school funding, blue ribbon status, their performance reviews, and microscopes for the science department were on the line. Caroline was paralyzed. Anxiety, as it usually did in these situations, took over. To keep the worst from happening, she wanted to make sure she followed the instructions from her teacher to the letter, guaranteeing her a good grade, and saving her from disappointing anyone if she failed. Through tears, she told me her teachers said they had to bring peppermints to help their brains.

"Help your brain?"

"Yes, my teacher said that peppermints make you smarter." (I am pretty sure the sugar in the peppermints will cancel out any of the smart ingredients.) In addition, I was supposed to write a letter telling Caroline how important the test was and how much we (her parents) were counting on her to pass the test. For a person with anxiety, this was torture. She wanted to follow the teacher's directions to the letter. She was trying to control the outcome, but when the only good outcome was perfection; it wasn't going to work. She needed to "take a risk."

The payoff for the risk needed to knock the anxiety out of her brain, assure her we loved her and that she could face down her fears of being imperfect. This is what I did. I bought her Mike and Ike's, her favorite candy at that age, and I wrote a note. It was to the effect, "Dear Caroline, this test means nothing. I don't care how you score. Do your best or not. I love you."

I wouldn't have written that note to any of my other children. There are some that would have read that note and decided they had permission to walk out and others that would have just been confused. But it was the only way I knew how to assure Caroline our love was not based on the results of that test. I knew if she could relax, she would do as she always does: ace the test. And she did, every year. The outcome of the test was a result of Caroline doing her best, whatever that was, and not from eating peppermints and my putting on additional pressure.

Effort (e)

Daily effort is amplified when driven by the energy that comes from the belief that what we do matters. It is this "purpose-driven effort" that is part of the formula. Purpose-driven effort drives the day and brings about growth and change in your life and in the lives of your children.

This daily effort will rarely be defined by large acts of service and sacrifice. It is in the small acts that our best work is done. These small acts leave a greater impact than anything you can manufacture or try to create: the conversations we have in the car; the smiles, hugs, and kisses just because; questions about something our child is interested in and our listening to the answers; teaching our children to read; playing a game; or telling jokes.

I would, on occasion, make cookies for my children. I would mix up the dough and then spread it all over the cookie sheet for the sake of time and simplicity. When the cookies were baked, I would cut them up into squares like you do with brownies. One day, my son William came home from school all excited. A friend brought "round" homemade cookies in his lunch.

"MOM!"

"Yes?"

"Did you know that cookies you make could be round like the cookies in the store?"

He was surprised to hear that, yes, I did know that. William asked why I didn't make round cookies. I explained that cutting them into squares made cookie making quick and easy. He asked under what circumstances would I make round cookies. I told him if I knew someone I loved was going through a hard time, or feeling sad, I would take my time and make them round for them. About a week after that conversation, I had the thought to make some cookies for the kids after school and decided to make them round. Will came home from school and ate the cookies. That evening, I found a note on my bed:

"Mom, thank you. You knew I had a bad day and made me round cookies so I would feel better. Love, William."

Looking back, there was nothing greater I could have done than the simple act of making my son some round cookies. In addition, a belief-focused effort can be pointed and specific to a predetermined end. There are times that what we don't know gets worked out through time. We have to learn that six-month-old babies knock books off the shelves, and they all scream when they don't get their way. Toddlers all run faster than we can, and even disappear in a blink of an eye. But other things like behavioral, health, or our own marital issues may require us to focus our efforts in seeking out new skills we need but do not have.

Knowing how to help Caroline through her anxieties did not just happen. Skills didn't miraculously manifest themselves when Caroline's anxieties did. At first, everything I said was wrong and seemed to make things worse. I began to read books, talk to a professional counselor, and reach out to friends. Once I learned how her brain worked and learned her language, I was able to help her better navigate her way through it.

Included in all of our efforts to grow and learn or develop new skills is a learning curve. Not even a purpose-driven and belief-focused effort can guarantee that we will get it right every time. In what the Lord knows to be a process, we sometimes feel we are letting Him and others down when we make a single mistake. The truth is, there will be mistakes. In a drawing class, my teacher said, "Drawing is not an action, it is a process. Part of the process involves coming to a visual understanding of what we are seeing or imagining and drawing." He went on to explain that this takes time and a lot of erasing. Both time and erasing are important components of mothering. Maybe you do yell too much, and maybe this morning you were impatient with your children. Be kind to yourself. Acknowledge that sometimes mistakes are made. In a conversation with my daughter-in-law, Jamie, she said, "I am learning that beating myself up isn't going to make my kids feel better. I just have to dust myself off and try again."

Recently, Caroline and I were going through what our family calls "Keep Forever Boxes." They are boxes that store different pictures and memories. I came across a note Caroline wrote to the Tooth Fairy:

"Dear Tooth Fairy, my tooth is under my pillow. Please leave money." To which I had written, "The tooth fairy needs to go to the bank." Although both Caroline and I laughed when we found the note, I knew that was not my best moment. I had quite a few "not my best moments." We all do.

We often forget that through our efforts, we can make things right and learn to do better. Instead, we follow ourselves around, pull out everything that was said or done, judge it at the end of the day when we are tired anyway, and punish ourselves for it every day after that. We spend so much energy trying to project this perfect image of what we know we aren't, when it would be so much easier to just accept that we are imperfect, and try to be better each day.

One day, when I was recounting a conversation/argument I had with one of my children to my husband, I concluded by saying, "I had it!" and proceeded to tell him the "insensitive" and "horrible" thing I had said to my sweet child. Hearing it out loud, I realized that although it wasn't the best thing I could have said, it wasn't really that bad either. My husband, Rich, surprised me by saying, "The best thing we can do when we mess up is put a nickel into their psychiatrist jar." Although he was speaking figuratively, and a little tongue-in-cheek, it helped me realize that no matter our good intentions, we aren't going to get it right every time. The next morning, the child I thought I had destroyed was happy. He still loved me. I told him I was sorry I acted impatiently and gave him a hug and kiss. The Psychiatrist Jar became a joke between Rich and me, a way to help keep things in perspective.

If we strive to be the best mother our children ever had, we can trust that with purpose-driven and belief-focused effort, the things we say and do that "aren't right" mix in with what we say and do that "is right." Our children, armed with their lists of "things I will never say to my children," have children of their own and will call you up one day because they have said the very things they swore they would never say. It's the circle of life.

The truth is that you are the only one who can be you. Always remember our formula:

$$io + ic + e = BME$$

Being the best mother your children ever had requires you to be exactly who you are, which requires a belief and faith in yourself, a faith that helps you know that when your children do things that you did not teach them to do, when they are trying to test the waters, when they tell you they don't love you, when you pray that someone else will take over, no one will love them more than you. Despite all of our imperfections, no one will do it better than you. To borrow a common phrase from the quantitatively inclined: math never lies.

CHAPTER TWELVE

The Sacredness of the Everyday

What "greater cause" could a member of the "royal generation" possibly be involved in?

I found myself in the bathroom, toilet-training my youngest child. He was sitting backwards on the seat and I was leaning over him, looking down into the toilet, "waiting." As I stood there, I thought about all the morning sickness I had had over seven pregnancies, the washing out of cloth diapers in the toilet, the bouts of stomach flu the kids each had, and all the time I spent looking down, "waiting," as I toilet-trained seven children. I worked it out in my head, and I think I figured I had spent 12 years of my life staring into a toilet.

Later, I began thinking about an experience I had at age 14. I attended a church meeting for the youth, ages 12-18. The speaker declared, "You are part of a royal generation." I remembered thinking at the time that sounded pretty important and must mean I was destined for great things in my future, *perfect* adult life. After all, when my teenage friends and I talked about being adults, we figured the hard part of life would be over. I mean, what did our mothers ever have to worry about?

I began to try and reconcile my teenage interpretation of that statement made so long ago with the fact that I had been staring down a toilet for 12 years. "Hmmm," the adult me thought, "I sure wish my youth leaders had given a more detailed explanation of what it means to be part of a 'royal generation.' Does it really include laundry piles taller than myself, or making an infinite amount of peanut butter sandwiches? How about more dirty diapers than any living person should have to deal with, and floors mopped in the morning that are filthy again after lunch? Does it include sullen teenagers, or midnight runs to Walmart for poster board and other essential items that absolutely could not wait until the next day?"

Given the day-to-day job description of motherhood, it is natural at times to wonder: "Is what I am doing going to make a difference in the life and in the progression of my family? At the end of my life, will the fact that I stared down a toilet for 12 years matter?" Some might reach the conclusion that their time and efforts would be better spent taking up what some might perceive as a "greater cause." But that's not true. These things we do, the daily chores of life in our homes at times may feel pointless, but there is a purpose and a sacredness to them.

"Families go back before the earth was and they will go forward into eternity."[27] These words speak to Heavenly Father's Plan of Salvation, also known as The Plan of Happiness. Faith in His plan requires movement on our part: getting up each day and going to work. When I go to the zoo, I often see the workers walking around in their muck boots. Families are messy and sometimes, we too have to put on our muck boots and wade in. But this in no way diminishes the importance of the work we do or the part these daily tasks play in His wonderful plan. What "greater cause" could a member of a "royal generation" possibly be involved in?

Our homes are hallowed ground.

Our homes are where our families pray, where our knees meet the ground. We pour out our hearts, express our sorrows, and share our feelings of gratitude, thus making our homes the most sacred of places. As with all hallowed ground, it must be watched over, protected and preserved as a place where the Lord's influence can be felt. Helaman, a prophet from The Book of Mormon, counseled his son on the importance of taking care of the sacred things with which the Lord has entrusted us.[28] As we clean our homes, beautify,

27 L. Tom Perry, "Why Marriage and Family Matter—Everywhere in the World," *Ensign*, May 2015. © By Intellectual Reserve, Inc.

28 *The Book of Mormon*. Salt Lake City: The Church of Jesus Christ of Latter-day Saints, 2013. Alma 37:14.

and create inside the walls, we are on hallowed ground. Those daily mother jobs, including the ones that need muck boots, help us take care of our sacred homes and, most sacred of all, our children, our families who live inside.

The everyday perfects us.

The Lord doesn't ask us to do anything that doesn't aid in the perfecting of our souls, enabling us to return to our Father in Heaven. All that we are asked to do in this life helps us in the next. Motherhood or nurturing is no exception. It changes us. We may not see it, but it is happening just the same. From the selfless service we render to our children, without any expectation of reward, comes eternal perspective, companionship of the spirit, peace, comfort, and the ability to love others more than ourselves. We learn more about ourselves. We learn how God sees us, and what He knows we are capable of doing. Every day, we learn to accept and recognize His grace in our lives. This perfecting has nothing to do with our children, their choices, or the theoretical outcome of parenting. Not every day, but on occasion, there will be times when we will see how far we have come and what the Lord accomplished while we thought we were just doing our laundry.

The everyday perfects our families.

When my children lived at home, they really couldn't have told you what I did every day. I say this with some certainty because occasionally, when they would get home from school, they would ask, "What do you do while we are in school and you have nothing to do?" (A direct quote.)

"What do you think I do?"

"Well, if we aren't here, you probably just sit and watch TV or do nothing." (Sigh.)

We wonder whether our children remember what we do if they don't even KNOW what we do. Once again, the question is: "Do the invisible things mothers do each day, the things that take up so much of our time and energy, matter? Will they matter in the life or the outcome of my children?"

To better answer this question, let's imagine that a tapestry is being woven, reflecting our life and our family. When a tapestry is being made, rarely do we see the whole picture. We know motherhood is sacred. We have all had those moments, rocking our babies to sleep in the middle of the night when the house is quiet, when we know that the work we do matters in this life and the next. But more often than not, we have to rely on our faith that what we do matters, knowing that the picture of motherhood is woven slowly, one string at a time.

There will be times though, that the tapestry comes into view and, for a moment, instead of seeing it with all its knots and random threads, we see the beautiful picture it has become.

The timing of Eric and Daniel's full-time missions for our church was such that Eric got home while Daniel was still out. By the time Daniel had gotten home, it had been three years since our family had all been together. Consequently, we got everyone together for a Christmas family reunion.

Our family reunions are always fun. (Spoiler alert: you think that things will calm down once your children grow up, but they don't. They just get bigger and louder). Typically, we can count on a few things. A debate usually breaks out between the children: the older three or four always like to point out how much harder their lives were before mom and dad "got old" and became so "lax," thus allowing the younger children to get away with "everything." The younger children will listen closely wanting to hear stories from a time in their childhood they don't remember.

We can always expect the phrase, "Remember the time when . . ." which leads into oft-repeated (and increasingly exaggerated) memories of fun family trips and heroic adventures. There are always discussions about injuries: the time Eric broke his arm or how many times Michael fell down the stairs. They laugh about the fights they used to have and games they used to play. They bring up their favorite Family Night memories of scripture charades, how Michael always chose "Help" by the Beatles for the opening song and Caroline always chose "My Heavenly Father Loves Me." Our family loves music and eventually, the guitars get pulled out and everyone sings along.

This reunion was no different. Immediately after congregating, we were laughing and enjoying ourselves. We told our inside jokes, quoted great movie lines, caught up on each other's lives, and recounted childhood memories like I just described.

On this occasion, while I was listening to the music and feeling such love for my family, my mind drifted and I thought about the various memories that were shared. I came to the realization that although the memories of fun were true, I had somewhat different perceptions of the same events.

My memories of the "fun family trips," included making sure clothes were washed, packed and loaded in the car, along with food and snacks. I spent time assembling dozens of sandwiches in the front seat of the car, changing diapers along the roadside, and taking children into dirty bathrooms. Their fights and games at home always led to holes in the drywall, scuffs on the floor, and messes to be picked up. Repeated requests that they stop rough-housing before someone got hurt almost invariably led to me fixing up someone who, in fact, got hurt. Family Home Evening took military-precision planning to get everyone into the same room at the same time. Dinner and homework had to be completed on time. Dessert had to be made or I had to help whomever was making it. Depending on the age of the child giving the lesson, help and follow-up was required.

The importance and sacredness of my perception of events made an impression on me as I combined my children's memories with mine. I finally had a glimpse of what had been woven over time and realized the vital part I played in creating such a beautiful picture.

Woven tapestries consist of two types of strings: horizontal and vertical. The horizontal strings vary in length, texture, and color. They form the picture. The vertical strings are neutral in color and invisible to the eye once the tapestry is woven, but they serve as the framework or skeleton of the picture.

In my family's tapestry, the horizontal threads were great days of color and adventure: family trips, playing together, and experiencing the joys and sorrows of life. The everyday routine that may at the time have seemed unimportant (changing diapers, washing dishes, endless laundry and some days, muck boots) can be compared to those vertical strings. They may not be mentioned or remembered, but they are holding the framework of our family together. It was those life errands and chores that helped us to learn to work together, appreciate each other, make memories that last, and love each other unconditionally.

The fact that the vertical strings can't be seen does not in any way make them less vital to the overall picture. If they were pulled out of a tapestry, the beautiful picture would tumble into an unrecognizable pile of strings and threads. Figuratively, throughout my family's life, both types of threads woven together, each dependent on the other, created a picture of a legacy of love and devotion binding us together in ways that cannot be undone.

As I look back on my nearly forty years of mothering, it makes me smile and cry tears of joy, firm in the understanding that our homes can be our holy ground, and what we do as mothers, from the easy and fun to the hard and messy, is important and has its own sacredness.

Every year, there are award shows and banquets to recognize the accomplishments of many people doing a variety of things. We might find ourselves wondering, "Where is my award? When will someone thank me for what I do?" But I will tell you, that night at the family reunion, I saw through spiritual eyes what had been accomplished through decades of what some call "thankless service" for my family. I wouldn't trade that precious moment of understanding from the Lord for anything the world has to offer. Although, I wouldn't mind if someone got those muck boots bronzed for me and placed them on the fireplace mantle.

CHAPTER THIRTEEN

A Mighty Work

"Remember whose you are, whose power is behind
you and the mighty work He has called you to do."

*A*t the beginning of the book, I wrote about the day my nest became empty. This wasn't the end of mothering, because there is no end, but the end of the days with a full house of children, schedules and all of the everyday experiences that accompany that time of life. And so, at the end of my book, I would like to go back to the beginning: the first step to a full nest.

Being a mother was always my dream job. I looked forward to the day when I would have children and always planned to have a large family. Regardless of my desires, I lacked practical "mothering" experience. I was not raised with a lot of little brothers and sisters and babysitting jobs were, for the most part, taking care of older children. And so, on the threshold of my becoming a mother, I realized I had a lot of questions.

I asked experienced mothers for help. In response, I got everything from "feed them condensed milk" to "dip the pacifier in honey." I actually did try the honey trick. When Melanie was a month old, I sat in horror as I listened to a news report warning parents not to give babies under age one raw honey. Evidently, honey can cause infant botulism, a rare but potentially fatal illness—awesome.

I read books written by people who had all sorts of initials after their names. I trusted that they knew what they were talking about and from there, formed a list of things that I learned.

1. If the baby is hungry, give her food. Put her on a schedule. A breastfed baby should eat every three hours; bottle fed, every four. (Great. I can set a timer!)
2. When the baby is awake, she will love time spent on her tummy, looking at her surroundings and enjoying life. It

149

was called, "tummy time." (Cool. I could do whatever I wanted while she lied happily on her tummy!)

3. Change her diaper often. (Obvious.)

4. Treat diaper rash with products like Desitin. (Ok. Got it. Purchase a year's supply.)

5. Weigh the pros and cons of using a pacifier. I decided to sacrifice the baby's perfect bite and pay the orthodontist later, being assured by the experts that letting the baby use the pacifier at will would help her calm down and/or fall asleep. The books assured me that after six months, I could simply take the pacifier away and she would never miss it!

6. Bathe the baby every other day. (Got it. I had a book with directions. It didn't look hard.)

7. Burp her after every ounce of milk, approximately. Doing so would prevent stomach aches that would keep her up all night. (This one became a high priority!)

This advice all seemed straightforward. I came to the conclusion that being a "good mom" was simple. I am an organized, schedule-loving person. Mothering was going to be right up my alley! All I had to do was do everything right, every day. I would follow a daily schedule and to-do list. Easy.

The day came and our first daughter, Melanie, was born into the world. After a three-day stay at the hospital, we were sent home, unsupervised by anyone who knew anything about how to care for this sweet bundle of joy. It was as if Melanie knew she was in the hands of amateurs. She cried all the way home from the hospital. I can't remember all the ways I tried to calm her, but I have a strong feeling the miracle of the pacifier did not manifest itself. We brought her into the house screaming. She messed in, under, around, and through her diaper. My hormones were at unsafe levels and as I sat down, trying to figure out what to do, I became overwhelmed and confused. Soon, both Melanie and I were crying.

My perfect plan fell apart. I had followed all of the advice, done what the books said to do. But there was not a chapter in any book I read that explained what to do when the baby didn't know the plan.

My belief in my abilities took a hit. I had done the research and I thought I was prepared. What I hadn't done was factor in the real life part of mothering. On that first day home, I had no idea what I would face and learn over four decades of mothering. I only knew that I had failed my first test. If could go back in time and talk to that young, overwhelmed mother, I would tell her:

1. Be kind to yourself.

I was sitting in church watching my granddaughter, Hannah, draw a self-portrait. She was nine years old and her medium was crayon. Not liking the way her nose turned out, she took a crayon and crossed it out with a big X. Afterwards, she immediately went back to work. I was curious at her lack of interest in or angst over the mistake she made. When she was done, I asked her if she liked her picture. A huge smile on her face answered the question. "Yes," she said, and began another drawing. Hannah didn't point out the mistake. Looking at the finished product, I saw a beautiful self-portrait reflecting the love Hannah had for herself and her innate ability to forgive a mistake.

When we are kind to ourselves, we accept what we can do and accept grace for what we cannot. Have faith in the Savior's grace, which he gives freely. "God is fully aware that you and I are not perfect."[29] There is only perfection through our Savior. We can trust in His atonement and in His ability to perfect us. My grandson, Justin, is serving a mission and wrote in one of his letters, "healing does not come literally after we do all we can do, it comes *while* we do

---

29 Dieter F. Uchtdorf, "Forget Me Not," *Ensign*, November 2011. © By Intellectual Reserve, Inc.

all we can do. We come to Christ in our weakness, and He carries us as we stumble on the path to perfection, until we don't stumble anymore." Nowhere does it say we must obtain perfection on our own, nor does God's plan for us on Earth require zero mistakes. Why should we put pressure on ourselves in ways that not even God requires? In the end, it will not be our mistakes that define us, but the lessons we learned along the way that will be reflected and become part of our self-portrait.

Look into a mirror every time you see one. Resist the urge to find fault with what you see. Instead, look at yourself and smile. I have a good friend who, in her efforts to be kinder to herself said, "I have been making myself pause and smile at myself. It actually feels really good, you know, after the first few awkward times." She pointed out that after a while, it was like the woman in the mirror was smiling back, encouraging her and telling her she was doing ok.

My daughter, Melanie, was driving down the road one day and her then five-year-old son, Jackson, said from the backseat: "When did I become so AWESOME?" At five, he understood that he is of great worth and has much to offer. What if, every time you looked at yourself in the mirror, you smiled and asked yourself, "When did I become so AWESOME?" (Say it like awesome is in all capital letters.)

When kindness starts with you, it will magnify your mothering and reduce the harsh judgments we make of others and ourselves. When applied, kindness can be a healing balm. Kindness can change the course of relationships with members of your family and with yourself. Kindness can calm angry waters, bring peace, assurance, and confidence. When we are kind to ourselves, we can better tap into that strength and face down a bad day.

Michael was home for a visit and I was having a particularly frustrating morning, driving every which way across town, facing delayed appointments, and scheduling conflicts galore. Michael, in an effort to comfort me, said, "Mom, this day is trying to take you down, but, you can't let it. You are stronger than this day."

Being a mother stretches us beyond our perceived capacities. We all get down on our knees and tell the Lord "no more," while at the same time getting up the next morning and doing it all over again. You prove every day that you are stronger than you think. Have faith in your capacity, abilities, and strengths that allow you to stare the day in the face and refuse to let it take you down.

Being kind to ourselves requires us to make friends with ourselves. Do what you would do to build a friendship. Get to know yourself, spend time with yourself. Take a walk, engage in the things that feed your soul. Ponder the gospel, the times in your life when you felt God's love. Ask your Heavenly Father to help you see yourself as He sees you. Kindness allows for a peace that whispers a message to our heart. It says, "You are enough." With that peace, we can bravely pick up our crayons and draw.

2. Embrace the good.

There are life-stopping events that happen to all of us. How to cope and deal with those kind of situations is a whole other book. But, in speaking of daily life, we can embrace the good as we put our challenging days into perspective.

To embrace something suggests that we like the whole of it. The word embrace implies the presence of good feelings, acceptance, and warmth. When our children were the age to begin choosing a spouse, they would often list out for us what they did and didn't like about someone they were dating. We would tell them, "before you decide to marry this person, you have to decide if you love the whole package, as if nothing was ever going to change." This is how we must embrace the good: our children's safety, the physical and emotional nurturing we give them, a particularly meaningful talk we had or a reverent family prayer. Those are not simply consolation prizes for an otherwise crummy day, if we truly embrace them warmly and wisely.

Have faith that what you do makes a difference. Who would imagine that our unremarkable family life, amidst all of our other endeavors and concerns, will bring us more real, lasting joy and eternal glory than anything else? But it is the labor of love we perform within the walls of our homes that will become the basis for our eternal glory. It can be challenging to believe or remember that mothering is part of a bigger eternal picture; we often arrive at the erroneous conclusion that what we do as mothers is not important, won't be remembered, or won't matter. As we embrace the good in our lives and put our faith in the great work we are doing, and in ourselves, we will realize that what we do is more important than what people remember. Our own lives are in debt to generations of anonymous women who did nothing more than live their ordinary lives, leaving a mark on the world, not by their name, but by their actions. Are we so different from them?

Embrace your creativity in whatever form it takes. Creativity is not constrained to the well-known, or what would be considered mainstream talents. Every woman has different talents, skills, and personality traits. Embracing the good within us means embracing those very individual ways we can nurture through our creativity. The beautiful part of creating is that our various, unique, and one-of-a-kind skills create for our children a unique, one-of-a-kind, deeply personal childhood. Some mothers sing goofy songs or make delicious meals. Other moms take their children on walks or read books. We can create smiles on the faces of our children and peace in our homes. There is no limit to how or what we can create if we embrace the uniqueness within us and use our powers for good.

When I was a child, I wanted to learn how to do ballet and I asked my mom if I could take classes. Not having money for classes, but knowing a bit about ballet, she cleared the family room of all our furniture and installed a ballet bar to teach me and my friends ballet. On hot summer days, when we would whine and tell her there was nothing to do, she would make homemade instruments from things we had around the house. In the hot garage, she would pass out the instruments, get us all playing along pretty much (give or take) the same beat, and send us out in parade fashion to march around the block a few times. To this day, one of our favorite shared memories is of a rainy day when she had me take out all of my Barbies, then she pulled out her sewing machine and we spent the day playing while she made outfit after outfit for my dolls from scraps of cloth and without any patterns.

Embrace the good. Don't just acknowledge it, but embrace it. Let your children see you laugh, let them see that you love yourself, give them memories that reflect who you are. I used to say to the children "remember who you are," and Rich would always add "and don't let it bother you." Although he said this with humor, let's not lose sight of the powerful message. Accept yourself and as you embrace the good in you, you will help your children embrace the good in themselves.

3. Find joy in the everyday.

I once gave a talk in a women's conference with the theme, "With Joy Wend Your Way." The phrase comes from a well know Latter-day Saint hymn, "Come, Come Ye Saints,"[30] written in dire circumstances when the pioneers were being tested and stretched beyond capacity. The hymn boldly declares "with joy, wend your way, all is well." I made note that the word joy comes first and it is with joy that we can wend our way through this life. Our capacity for joy doesn't require us to dismiss the fact that life is hard and we will

---

30 William Clayton, "Come, Come, Ye Saints," 1846.

face challenges. True joy can really only be found in the middle of the difficulties. If we can learn to embrace the sacredness of now and accept that it is our job to act and not be acted upon, we can find joy despite our challenges. How do we recognize the sacredness of now when it isn't always apparent?

On a spring day in Indiana, I took Caroline and Michael with me to the plant nursery and bought some flowers for one of the beds in the front of the house. When we got home, I put Michael down for a nap and Caroline came out with me to "help me plant flowers." She kept putting them in the ground upside down or pulling out ones I had already planted. My looks of frustration were met with the words, "I am helping you," followed by her smiles and laughter. She was happy to be with her mother, digging in the dirt. Failing to recognize this sacred moment, my thought was, "I can't wait for the day that I can just plant flowers all by myself." Immediately, I heard the whisperings of the spirit: "Be careful. The time will come soon enough and you will wish you had little hands helping you again." Now, Caroline has children of her own, and decades have passed in what seems like a blink of an eye, and I do miss the little hands that loved to help. How grateful I am for the prompting that I was missing a sacred moment. That day is like a photograph in my mind and I remember my frustration being replaced with joy as I stayed in the sacred place of "now."

The sacredness of now requires that we keep our focus on the current moment. But as the days' events unfold, we can be so focused on what can go wrong or what has gone wrong that we don't see what has gone right. It is so easy for us to fail to accept the opportunity to act rather than to be acted upon by the day's twists and turns.

Caroline was home after her sophomore year of college. She and I went to the store. While in the produce department, she ate a piece of pineapple that came from a sample bowl. It got caught in her throat and she could not breathe. I can still see clearly as if it was yesterday, her looking at me, unable to speak, her face turning red, tears running down her cheeks, with eyes that were yelling, "help!" My feeble attempts at the Heimlich didn't work. Another woman tried, it did not work. A man (I found out later that he was a doctor) came up and after a few attempts, was able to dislodge the pineapple piece. I hugged Caroline close and told her she was absolutely grounded from eating pineapple. Ever. Again.

As we walked around the store, buying the groceries on our list as if nothing had happened, I allowed the "what ifs?" to creep in. "What if no one was able to help her? What if she had died? Then, of course it was my fault. I should have taken CPR classes. Why didn't I have my Heimlich maneuver certificate? I am a terrible mother. Who allows her child to choke on pineapple?" I was filled with worry and guilt.

Joy in the everyday is hard to achieve if we spend our time concentrating on all that could go wrong, and we run the risk of being so caught up in what might happen that we miss what is happening now.

We found ourselves in the same checkout lane as the doctor who had helped her. I thanked him again and I told him I was glad he decided to come shopping today. He stopped, got a smile on his face and explained. He had not planned to go to the store that day, but the idea came to him that he should. He now understood that it was no stray thought, but a direction by a greater power to be at the right place at the right time.

The "what ifs?" melted away when I started concentrating on what went right instead of what went wrong. Gratitude and faith began to replace worry and guilt. The Lord, in anticipation of the events that would take place, got the right person there at the right time. I acknowledged the blessing that Caroline did not die and that it was not my fault that the pineapple got stuck. Although I was not successful in helping Caroline myself, I asked for help and found the very person who was sent there to help her. Faith, gratitude and the knowledge of my Savior's presence in that moment helped me appreciate the sacredness of now. Acknowledging the blessings in even the most unfortunate events, looking for the tender mercies, and refusing to play the blame-ourselves game, allows us to feel joy.

Once again, my thoughts turn to my first step into motherhood. The day I took Melanie home, I went very quickly from thinking I knew all the answers to feeling overwhelmed with fear and doubt at the realization that in fact, I knew nothing. I couldn't have known that that day I thought was so hard would in fact, once put into perspective, seem simple and easy when compared to other days.

I know how hard it is to do what I am suggesting you do. I wish I could tell you that if you do, birds will sing, children will be obedient, and all disasters and challenges will disappear like fluffy clouds, but I can't. Doubts, comparisons, and times of feeling overwhelmed come in and crowd out our good intentions. In addition, the real part of life intrudes and threatens to dismantle us down to our souls. I know that so many of you carry the weight of unbearable challenges. Sometimes, the weight of our challenges becomes too much. We grow weary of saying the same prayers over and over while feeling as if the problems we are praying about never get resolved. The words in the scriptures start to ring hollow and get lost in the noise of the world. The once harmonious strands of the gospel that were easy to pick out become faded, distant, or seemingly out-of-date as we trade them in for the newer, louder, and sometimes more exciting notes of today.

As challenging as your days and circumstances are, as enticing as the world seems, and as far away as the Lord feels at times, you are never alone. Remember whose you are, whose power is behind you and the mighty work He has called you to do.

Can you imagine what might happen if we smiled in every mirror we saw, telling ourselves we are doing our best and that we are enough? What if we became the kind of friend we are to others, to ourselves? What if we walked away from any perception of a perfect image and embraced the good in ourselves while working with the Lord on our weakness? What if we all strived to find joy in the everyday, recognizing the sacred moments along the way? What would that army of women look like? We would see women stamping out negative thoughts and showing up for work with all their superpowers, ready to go, being kind to themselves and embracing their individuality, knowing that their unique skills and talents aren't just enough; they are essential. This is my wish for me, for you, for all of us.

I would love for every woman to lift each other up and celebrate their differences. I would love for every woman to greet each morning looking for the joy she will find in today and embracing the good when the day ends. I would love for every woman to feel, in the depths of her soul, the love her children have for her, even on her self-proclaimed worst days. I would love for every woman to hear the silent shouts of her children that say, "I need you," even when they slam the door yelling "I hate you!" I would love for every woman to know that as she places her trust in the Savior, He will give her the strength to overcome any challenge she has to face and be mightier than any mountain she has to climb. I would love for every woman to guard the gate of her home, making it a haven in the storm, for herself and her family, knowing there is no better place to stand.

Made in the USA
Columbia, SC
01 August 2019